SONGWRITING
in PRACTICE
NOTEBOOKS • JOURNALS • LOGS • LISTS

T0066147

Mark Simos

Berklee Press

Editor in Chief: Jonathan Feist
Senior Vice President of Online Learning and Continuing Education/CEO of Berklee Online: Debbie Cavalier
Vice President of Enrollment Marketing and Management: Mike King
Vice President of Online Education: Carin Nuernberg
Editorial Assistants: Emily Jones, Megan Richardson
Cover by Ranya Karafilly
Photographer: Louise Bichan

ISBN: 978-0-87639-190-7

Berklee
Press

1140 Boylston Street
Boston, MA 02215-3693 USA
(617) 747-2146

Visit Berklee Press Online at
www.berkleepress.com

Berklee Online

Study music online at
online.berklee.edu

DISTRIBUTED BY

HAL•LEONARD®
7777 W. BLUEMOUND RD. P.O. BOX 13819
MILWAUKEE, WISCONSIN 53213

Visit Hal Leonard Online
www.halleonard.com

Berklee Press, a publishing activity of Berklee College of Music, is a not-for-profit educational publisher.
Available proceeds from the sales of our products are contributed to the scholarship funds of the college.

CONTENTS

PREFACE AND ACKNOWLEDGMENTS

This book represents the fruits of many years of my own practice as a songwriter and co-writer, as well as a teacher of songwriting and a reflective practitioner. As I worked on the book, I revisited the history of many songs written, becoming ever more fascinated with how other songwriters, and artists of all kinds, manage their creative work. This book represents a next step in an evolving body of shared experience and practice. I hope to follow up with case studies, interviews, and new exercises and challenges, via resources such as my songwriting website *www.360songwriting .com* and blog *The Songwriter's Compass*, and my artist's website *www.devachan.com.*

I've been privileged to co-write with many great songwriters. For contributions and insights reflected in this book, I am especially grateful to those co-writers—Lisa Aschmann, Jon Weisberger, and Scarlet Keys, among many others—who have also joined with me in inquiry into songwriting practice and process, through our thoughtful conversations in and around co-writing sessions.

Many of my students have also acted as enthusiastic fellow researchers, working with many of the tools and practices described in this book. I'd like to thank especially Lily Lyons for her field trials of Appointments with Inspiration, and Talia Segal for field-testing the "seed rescue" operation. Megan Richardson served both as student experimenter, and later as an editorial assistant.

Jonathan Feist was my editor for *Songwriting Strategies*, and has continued as a great mentor and writing teacher as well as editor for this project. In addition, several of his own books cover topic areas highly complementary to the scope of this book. *Project Management for Musicians* (Berklee Press, 2013), particularly, provides general project and task management principles, for many practical aspects of the music business.

For references scattered throughout the book, I'd like to thank: Lisa Aschmann for sharing with me Steve Leslie's three rules, Cathy Fink for "purpose vs. play," Nora Brown for her thought-provoking questions about the Red Notebook, Evie Ladin for "just collect," Suzanne Hamstra for "meaty fresh," Danny Carnahan for his term "fragment file" for my Stewpot, Eileen Carson for "making a practice," Kathy Hussey for "ruthless revisers," Janet Peterson for the "first song you learned" prompt for Songs I Wish I'd Written, Jon Weisberger for clarifying the Gallery of Horror rules—and Eden and Lukas Pool for donating their wedding celebration to Songwriting Science.

CHAPTER 1

Introduction: Songwriting as a Practice

In the summer of 2017, I took a trip to Nashville for the epic annual birthday party of my long-time co-writing "sister of song" Lisa Aschmann. (You'll hear more about her later.) When I described this book to her, she laughed and shared with me the admirably terse advice (three maxims, nine words total) that songwriter Steve Leslie usually gives to up-and-coming songwriters:

1. Write great songs.
2. Move to Nashville.
3. Feed the poor.

I laughed, in turn, because, as I thought about it, I realized that the focus of this book is precisely the stuff that falls between the cracks of these three areas of concern. It's about what's *between* the art (or at least, craft) and the business aspects of songwriting: the mundane yet critical regular activities, tools, and consistent places to put stuff. It's what songwriters *do* when they write songs. These "housekeeping" details are less often discussed or written about than the craft or business aspects, and can easily get passed over as you wrestle with deeper aesthetic or more urgent professional issues. Yet, they provide an essential foundation on which to build a sustainable professional presence as a songwriter. And how you manage these details can also have surprisingly profound effects on the quality of your creative work itself.

In this book, I aim to address these housekeeping aspects: how you organize your song ideas (what I call "song seeds") and source material; how you format and maintain seed lists and journals, drafts, versions, revisions, demos, and pitch sheets; how you keep track of co-write sessions; and how you manage your overall catalog.

CREATIVE WORKFLOW IN SONGWRITING

To be a little more technical, and general, we can say the practice of songwriting includes all the ways you manage your *creative workflow*: all the materials you produce in the course of writing and demoing songs and getting them out into the world in various forms and channels, and the activities involved in working with these materials.

We could say Steve's three maxims concern, respectively, the *craft*, the *business*, and the *ethics* or *purpose* of songwriting. Adopting a more coherent and disciplined approach to creative workflow management supports—in fact, is essential to—each of these aspects of your songwriting practice as a whole. To clarify these interconnections, let's look first at how songwriting workflow management links craft and business concerns. (We'll come back to the ethics, feeding the poor, at the end of this introduction.)

Write Great Songs

How to write great songs is, of course, the subject matter of an extensive industry and literature on songwriting *craft*: skills, techniques, and aspects of songs that lend themselves to commercial success. I've written one myself that I think is pretty good: *Songwriting Strategies: A 360° Approach* (Berklee Press, 2014). The songwriting approach I describe in that book offers a new, comprehensive, and holistic model encompassing the diverse creative elements and processes involved in songwriting: lyrical as well as musical aspects, and their manifold interconnections.

To cover all that new technical ground, however, I had to leave unaddressed many pragmatic questions of managing all this material. For example, some heavy lifting happens in the middle chapters: "What does it really mean to start a song from melody? Once you have a melodic seed *that you have decided to work on*, what are the different strategies you can apply to develop that seed into a full song?"

Notice that hand-wavy phrase, "*that you have decided to work on.*" It's an almost cinematic cheat: "Catch seed . . . now dissolve to songwriter starting to work on seed . . . ." Yes, it's empowering to realize you can catch and develop song seeds at different times. But where do you keep seeds once you catch them? How do you organize them (if at all)? How do you decide *which* seeds to work on next, or *when* and *where* you'll buckle down and work on that seed—or on any seed?

The focus of this book is everything in that fuzzy bit during the dissolve: the creative *workflow management* part of the puzzle.

Steve's right: if you aren't writing great songs, or at least working steadily at writing better songs, nothing else really matters. But in this book, I'll steer away from extensive discussions of craft—techniques and forms of songwriting, ways of getting inspired, what makes a great or commercially viable song, etc. I'll assume you are putting regular energy into developing your craft, whether simply writing a lot, working with co-writers and/or a writer's group, participating in classes, workshops, or retreats, getting professional critiques, etc.

As you work on your craft, though, you will generate *a lot* of creative material. The curious thing is that handling that material is in many ways a separate set of concerns and skills from *how* you write songs. In fact, the better you get at the craft, the more productive you will be—and the more creative workflow you will need to manage.

For example, it's said that good writers *rewrite*. That means for every finished song, there is a substantial paper (and digital, and audio) trail left behind that you must eventually deal with. When you can't access that material effectively, you risk losing good ideas in a cloud of confused drafts, frustrating a co-writer, or sending out a stale demo version. Workflow management skills are how you integrate inspiration and craft into a true songwriting *practice*. Furthermore, managing creative materials more effectively also provides a wealth of information that you can draw and reflect upon, to continually advance your songwriting craft in profound ways.

Move to Nashville

While Steve may have meant "move to Nashville" literally, we can broaden his recommendation here to address, more generally, what we might call the business of being a songwriter. Along with books about the craft, many books deal with the business side of songwriting: copyrighting and registering songs, pitching material, negotiating a publishing or artist deal, building your website, and promoting yourself via social media.

Just as I am steering away from craft discussions in this book, I also will not discuss many specific, more outward-facing business aspects of songwriting. Besides being addressed in many other resources (such as *Making Music Make Money*, by Eric Beall; Berklee Press, 2003), these business aspects will tend to change quickly over time, and the specifics are highly dependent on particular industry markets and niches.

Songwriting as a core skill can now be deployed in a wide variety of media markets. You might be a performing singer-songwriter, primarily focused on writing for yourself and performing your own songs; a band member, collaborating with others to write for your band; a project writer focused on song "synch" (-ronization) placements for film, television, Web, video games, or virtual reality communities; a producer/writer writing for and with other artists; or (though this model sadly seems to be on the wane) a staff writer or independent writer, writing and co-writing songs to pitch to artists and projects via a publishing company or an independent song plugger.

Each of these scenarios requires distinct business practices, ways of dealing with your audience and/or your customers, products, contracts, and projects. These business aspects will also change rapidly, as the music industry continues to undergo inevitable revolutions, destructive innovations, and upheavals in coming years.

The need to manage creative workflow effectively, though, is common to all these scenarios. Every successful business outcome is supported by workflow management. When you sign a publishing deal, you need an accurate inventory of your catalog. To pitch songs in a timely fashion to artists or for projects, you need some way of searching that catalog for good prospects. As this is primarily *inward-facing* work—your own way of keeping track of things for yourself—your own style and predilections will be a primary determinant of how you shape your routines, work products, and practices.

As is true of progress in your craft, achieving greater success at the professional level will only *intensify* your need for sound workflow management practices. The more opportunities you get to respond to and the faster you need to respond—the more projects you take on and juggle simultaneously—the more you will need to be managing.

Manage Your Workflow

The craft, the workflow management, and the business of songwriting form a powerful triad. You need to work on all three, but workflow management forms the connective tissue that integrates your practice as a whole:

FIG. 1.1. Skills of Songwriting

Some techniques I describe here might strike you as more detailed than necessary, given the current extent of your own catalog and your productivity as a songwriter. It may feel a bit like overkill—even slightly presumptuous—to set up those procedures and practices at this stage. But you will benefit greatly by adopting practices now that will prove sustainable over the long haul of your writing career. As you get better at the craft and the business, you ratchet up expectations, and the capacity your overall creative workflow needs to carry and sustain. At that point, it is difficult to set up new systems or learn new work habits. You'll want regular practices, tailored and adapted to fit your creative and working style, already in place. Your housekeeping skills will be a limiting factor on your capacity, for both inward-facing craft and outward-facing professional work.

You might think focusing on these practical skills can come later, after your first few albums and tours as an artist, or after landing your first cuts. In fact, these skills can make a critical difference in your getting those early lucky breaks, and sustaining that luck. Responding promptly to a project opportunity requires business discipline, but being able to search quickly through a list of pre-compiled ideas to get to the perfect starting point for a strong creative response depends on your workflow management skills. As the saying goes (attributed to any number of golfers), "The harder I practice, the luckier I get."

WHO CAN USE THIS BOOK?

I believe songwriting is creative activity that is or should be accessible to everyone, playing a role in every aspect of our personal, family, local community, and social lives. You can write songs for no reason other than your own enjoyment or spiritual growth. You can write songs to sing to your babies, for your family, to help your farm work, or to make a long drive go more quickly. In the long history of humanity, the vast majority of songs ever written, composed, improvised, sung, or played have happened in this way—just part of life and culture.

This book, however, is addressed to people prepared to do a fair amount of practical work to support their songwriting— who want to establish a songwriting *practice*. You have to have a reason to do all that work! This book should be useful to you if songwriting is integral, in some way, to work you do, whether professionally (for a living, or at least for money), or as a *calling*. So I'll assume you are a serious, practicing, and (at least aspiring) professional songwriter, in the following senses:

- You are writing songs with the intent to see them go "out into the world" in some way. (That's the professional part.)

- You want to do this as a continuing practice in your professional life, not just as a one-time life project. (That's the serious part.)

- You are also motivated to keep improving as a songwriter, as part of doing this work. Thus, you are willing to manage not just your songs, but also materials, debriefs, and reflections to fold back into the ways you write songs, to keep moving toward becoming the songwriter you mean to be. (That's the serious, and also the practicing part.)

NEED FOR THIS BOOK

It's frankly a curious thing, even to me, that the material in this book hasn't been written about that much in other sources. Could it be that, besides knowledge of songwriting craft and some business savvy, the main other ingredient of creative workflow management is simply good general organizational skills?

Of course, most songwriters (including me!), being creative types, would probably not rate themselves too highly on the "organized" scale! But, in fact, the problem is far trickier than that. If we look more closely at what is really being "managed" in the workflow of songwriting, it turns out to be unlike the kinds of materials and activities of typical project management or business organization. Creative material is—well, different.

Linking Inspiration and Opportunity

If you are a serious, practicing, professional or aspiring-professional songwriter in the senses outlined above, you can think of your creative work as a kind of arc, stretching between two poles: *inspirations* and *opportunities*.

- At the inspiration end are your starting points for songs. Once you move beyond writing songs only on impulse—as responses primarily to your personal emotional experiences—an essential part of your practice involves regularly scanning for inspirations and ideas for songs.

- At the opportunity end, you are similarly scanning for ways for your songs to be heard, performed, and recorded, whether by you as performing songwriter and artist or by other artists. More broadly, an opportunity is the world asking for a song—not a particular song (yet), but a need, a possible *placement*—for a film or television soundtrack, perhaps for a specific scene or title; or to celebrate or commemorate a person or event; or a request; or our own initiative, to write a song for a social or charitable cause.

If you don't care whether your songs ever get heard, you don't need an elaborate workflow management system. Conversely, if your creative work is primarily in response to direct work assignments, you may not need to manage lots of independent "inspirations" and connect them to those writing tasks. (For example, work done by advertising agency creative teams tends to be so focused on immediate, specific client requirements that their work processes may likely be very different from those described in this book.)

Most working songwriters, however, are constantly negotiating and trying to integrate these two poles of creative energy and focus. We initiate some songs in response to inspirations, others in response to opportunities. We look for opportunities for our songs, and songs for our opportunities.

Successful career songwriters learn to work from both directions, and you need both strategies to do either effectively. When you wake up with an idea for a song, that's inspiration at work. But eventually, you will look for an opportunity to "place" that song—to get it out into the world. A song idea that could go in a number of directions seems like a good potential pitch for an artist you know is looking. Out of many possible paths you could take with that song, you head toward that goal—hopefully not stressing the original idea in too awkward or contrived a direction. Conversely, you get a request from a publisher for songs for an artist or band, or for a specific project—an opportunity sparking you into action. You produce genuine, authentic material by connecting that task to inspiration, fulfilling the assignment with work that still feels personal and spontaneous to you. At that point, being able to search effectively through prior, archived, inspiration-based work may be key to working successfully, at the right pace and level of responsiveness—provided that the inspiration you find is truly a good fit for the opportunity.

Responding to opportunities without being able to tap into an archive of creative material risks making you purely reactive in your professional work. This is when professional songwriters can experience burnout from pressures of creative work becoming too driven, rather than shaped and channeled, by pitching songs to artists, or the production pressures of touring artists needing that next album's worth of material. Yet, being too beholden to the rhythms and serendipity of inspiration-based work, without linkage to opportunities, can also grow stultifying and stale. You may become a miser sitting alone in your counting house.

Creative workflow management is the essential "switching station" by which you effectively link inspirations and opportunities. It enables you to activate your inspirations as professional assets, and to enliven your responses to business opportunities with your full creative energies.

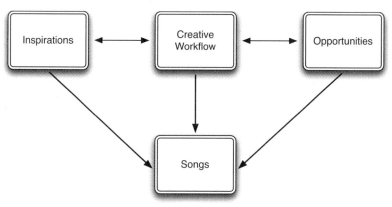

FIG. 1.2. The Endeavor of Songwriting

The Songwriting Endeavor

What sorts of tools and systems do we need to manage this creative workflow between inspirations and opportunities? Anyone managing complex, multitask projects can avail themselves of numerous resources and methods for project, task, and workflow management. Some of these organizational methods even address the interactions and delicate balance between work and personal life and priorities.

Part of creative workflow management involves linking songwriting activities with specific projects and tasks that are part of your professional work. But, while your workflow will dovetail with very different business tasks at the back end, and might be implemented with varying kinds of support technologies, applications, and media, the fundamental nature of that underlying creative workflow stays relatively constant.

Here, though, we must confront the fact that the nature of this workflow does not look much like a conventional project—either in writing an individual song, or at the global level managing your overall songwriting practice. The central problem is that mysterious creative entity, the heart and point of it all: the song. It's just not very helpful to treat writing a song as a rational project that can be broken down into linear steps, or to approach your songwriting work overall as a series of tiny projects.

Rather, we could say your songwriting practice is One Big Project—your complete catalog and life's work, which you work on, and will keep working on, for the duration of your creative and professional life. Since it's not a project in a conventional sense, I call this baseline of creative activities your *songwriting endeavor.* Whatever else you are doing—touring or making albums as an artist; pitching songs to other artists; getting songs placed in film, television, Web series, or AI-generated post-apocalyptic sci-fi multimedia podcasts—those tasks, projects, and opportunities all take place in the context of this overarching creative endeavor: finding sources of inspiration, turning them into songs, and connecting songs with opportunities.

Creative Workflow vs. Project and Tasks

Songwriters, due to their intertwined roles as professional musicians and artists, or responding to specific opportunities, certainly do have work projects and tasks in more conventional terms. Performing artists must book tours, show up at gigs, make albums at hopefully regular intervals, pursue opportunities to collaborate, etc. Producer-writers must cultivate relationships with artists, pitch songs, and respond promptly to pitch opportunities. Much of this business-as-usual and project work *is* more amenable to standard task and project management systems and tools—with a little tweaking, of course, to suit our rebel songwriter personalities.

In some situations, in fact, you can even treat writing a song as a sort of project. In its essence, the work of turning an idea into a song is inherently indeterminate and open-ended. However, once you say yes to an opportunity and commit to delivering creative work to requirements or on a schedule, it does become a project you need to manage, albeit one involving highly focused creative work. Task-based creative work *feels* different than work initiated from inspiration. For one thing, there are usually associated requirements, constraints, and time limits. Some songwriters love this kind of task-based work; others abhor it. Songwriter Cathy Fink nicely describes the tension between these modes of creative work as "play vs. purpose."

This interleaving of creative workflow and task management is not confined, by the way, only to staff or "project" writers. A songwriter may be focused on writing and performing their own material; but when they need to get songs together for that uphill-climb second album, while still touring non-stop for their first—believe me, that will feel like *task-based* writing.

As we explore later in this book, there are also ways to make inspiration-based work more like task work. Songwriters who "go to work each day" and write songs in an office from 9 to 5 are treating songwriting like a task—really, a job. In a more limited way, by creating regular practices for engaging with otherwise inherently unruly material such as song seeds (e.g., the Appointment with Inspiration discussed in chapter 4), you can, in effect, "task-ify" work from inspiration-based sources, making it more amenable to planning, scheduling, and integration into larger projects and work rhythms.

Overall, though, the focus of this book will be primarily on the creative workflow management part of songwriting practice. Just as aspects of craft and outward-facing business are beyond our scope, I will try to avoid replicating here advice and suggestions that are best covered as part of well-established project management and general organizational methods.

FIG. 1.3. Creative Workflow Management vs. Project/Task Management

SHARING PRACTICE

Even if songwriting presents some unique workflow management challenges, you might think that, by now, these would be well established and documented, even time-worn. Surely, Beethoven, Stephen Foster, Irving Berlin, and Smokey Robinson had to figure all this out!

Though I've had some moderate success as a songwriter, what I believe suits me well to the task of documenting these practices are some attitudes and approaches I've applied throughout my career.

Songwriters' Lore

In most informal fields of practice, practitioners learn from the previous generation through direct personal contact: that's what the apprenticeship system in various crafts and industries is (or used to be) about. Songwriting was, until recently, largely a "folk art" (even popular music songwriting!). Most great songwriters of the past did not study a formal songwriting pedagogy in settings such as college programs; they got their on-the-job training as working *musicians*, absorbing songwriting skills and knowledge by steeping themselves in the repertoire and performance practice of their genre or style.

In some songwriting traditions, such as an earlier generation of country music songwriters, apprenticeship of a sort also happened through *co-writing*. It was by sitting shoulder to shoulder with a more experienced writer that you picked up the tricks of the trade. (It's now becoming more difficult, unfortunately, to "apprentice" as a songwriter in this way.) This was essentially an oral tradition—what you might call the "folk practice" of songwriting. It didn't get written down—other than in stray comments in interviews, by and large directed towards fans, not up-and-coming songwriters.

I've written this book as if coaching an apprentice, explaining my own system in as much detail as I can. And, though I haven't made an exhaustive survey of different songwriters' ways of managing creative workflow, I've picked up a lot of "songwriters' lore" along the way, and have done my best to pass along some of those tools (and tricks) of the trade in this book.

A Scalable Practice

I am a very productive songwriter. I generate a *lot* of creative material. I work fast. Because I've trained myself to catch seeds as a regular practice, even at very busy times (when I probably *should* be doing something else!), I am at least capturing ideas for songs to work on later. The result is a very large archive of material, of widely varying granularity and degrees of completion, that I've had to learn to manage effectively.

And I've been at it a while. I'm over sixty, and have journals and music exercise books dating from about age eleven; that's about fifty years of creative output. In that sense, my own practice represents a kind of extreme test case.

What I describe in this book, therefore, will definitely *scale up*. Some of the practices I describe here are things experienced songwriters only learn once they have a significant body of work to keep track of. And some may be practices that successful songwriters *wish* they had in place!

This was brought home for me as I worked on honing this book's concept and focus and began discussing it with fellow songwriters—especially my "pro" writer friends, many of whom I look up to as models of being on top of things. Their immediate response, no matter how veteran, how successful, how presentably collected they appeared to be, was: "Wow! *I* need that book!" It seems that every songwriter wrestles with these pragmatic problems—quite apart from the eternal artistic struggles of writing a great song, telling your own truth, and impressing that cute audience member in the front row. And the more active and successful you are, the more you need to attend to the practicalities.

Reflective Practice

I also trained myself early on to be fairly reflective about my own practice. Some of this is just my nature and temperament: I'm kind of a theory nerd and a process maven, influenced by philosophies of technical work that advocate integrating reflection into work practice. For about twenty years, during the first half of my professional songwriting life, my day job was working in software technology as a "methodologist"—turning informal software practices into more formal methods. (I like to say that I spent my earlier career teaching systematic, technology-oriented people—engineers—to be more creative . . . and I now find myself encouraging creative people—like songwriters!—to be a little more systematic.)

My interest in artistic process came into its own when I joined Berklee's Songwriting faculty, where I've now taught for over a decade. To teach creative arts, I believe you must be able to look students in the eye and testify that you've done your own homework, and you've used and lived by—with at least some success—the methods you are espousing. That has forced me to be even more deliberate about examining my own processes, documenting and being able to explain them.

Field Trials

Perhaps most importantly, through my teaching work, I have had the privilege and benefit of working with hundreds of student songwriters at a formative period in their own writing careers, when habits and practices are first adopted that are likely to last. My observations and conversations, and the exercises and challenges I've developed working with these talented and dedicated students, have served as "field trials" for many of the practices suggested in this book. I've heard as much about problems as victories, and many ideas here are responses to recurring reports of the practical issues that plague writers.

Over time, I've worked and at times struggled to refine and evolve my own practice, and have come to terms with its being a constant work in progress. As a result, I am less fanatical that I have the "right" system—even for me. In this book, I avoid prescribing a one-size-fits-all approach, a rigidly defined set of songwriting "best practices." Where I do ground discussions with illustrations from my own work, these are provided not as prescriptions but as concrete examples of at least one way to do it, accompanied by some description of underlying rationale for the practice. You will of course not want to do things exactly as I do them. Use this book, instead, as a guide to the *questions* you want to be asking, in inquiring into and evolving your own practice.

WHAT'S IN THE BOOK

Underlying the many different ways songwriters manage creative material are a fundamental set of principles, practices, activities, and containers, as timeless in their way as a great song. Articulating these principles in actionable ways is my goal in writing this book—and the reason I hope it will stay timeless as well, and will wind up well-thumbed and dog-eared on your shelf—along with your thesaurus, rhyming dictionary, and other perennial sources of inspiration.

Flow and Format

Given our focus on managing the creative workflow of songwriting, this book is structured in a way that mirrors that flow: from the first inspiration and inception of songs, to their final form as finished demos, album tracks, and copyrighted documentation.

- **Managing Creative Workflow**. In chapter 2, we lay out key concepts of creative workflow that we will refer to in all the stages to come. We discuss problems of maintaining boundaries between different aspects of your creative work, and the roles of different kinds of containers (implemented both by various work products and supporting activities) in negotiating those boundaries.

- **Seeds and Sources**. In chapter 3, we discuss managing the initial materials that serve as inspirations for your songs. Such material can be partitioned, roughly, into *stuff you make up*—seeds, drafts, etc.—and *stuff you collect from outside sources* that you make use of in less direct ways in the course of writing songs. In chapter 4, we discuss supporting activities and practices for the work products that serve as containers for these materials.

- **Writing Songs**. In chapter 5, we move on to the creative work of developing seed and source material into songs. This involves accessing seed material, and creating sketches and drafts in multiple formats, including lyrics on paper, lead sheets, chord charts and diagrams, and computer text and audio files. In chapter 6, we discuss how to manage successive revisions of songs, and also how to receive and process *critiques* from various sources, to take your song forward.

- **Collaboration.** In chapter 7, we extend workflow management practices beyond solo work to accommodate collaborative work and co-writing.

- **Finalizing the Song.** In chapter 8, we finish discussion of workflow management for individual songs by looking at what is involved in finalizing, "fixing" a song into a final form.

- **Catalog Management.** In chapter 9, we step back to look at your entire catalog in light of the creative workflow steps explored so far. There are legal aspects to be considered here, including registering your work for copyright at the appropriate time and in the appropriate way, and arranging for administration of active copyrights. But the broader issues involve seeing your overall catalog as a management of flows between the fruits of *inspiration*—your songs— and various *opportunities*—invitations from the world to pitch songs to artists or various projects, or extending to your own work as a performing artist.

- **Reflective Practice.** Lastly, in chapter 10, we discuss a key, if less direct, aspect of songwriting workflow: supporting reflection on your practice, and channeling that learning into improved skills. This includes practices you may want to integrate directly into your creative work, such as left page/right page generative and reflective work formats. It also includes standing lists you can maintain, not tied directly to creative work (as are your song seed lists), but which you can use to spark new creative work and keep advancing your craft.

Resources in the Book

Given this roadmap of the stages of the song and songwriting life cycle we'll cover in this book, here is a look at the types of resources I'll suggest in each stage:

1. **Tools: Documents, spreadsheets, lists, annotations, conventions.** Whether working primarily on paper or on a laptop, on a mobile device or in a hand-bound parchment diary with a gold-embossed cover, managing creative workflow means creating various materials and recording

them. Having a clear concept of what kinds of documents are useful will help you get out in front of your creative work. For example, a lyric sheet may seem like a very simple idea—a text file with the lyrics to your song. But depending on what stage of writing you are at, whether or not you are working with a co-writer, whether you are providing a lyric sheet for a demo vocalist or studio engineer, etc., will dramatically affect the conventions and format you use. These resources are essentially various sorts of *containers* you set up and maintain to hold creative work in various stages of progress.

2. **Practices**. A *practice*, for our purposes, is simply a regular activity you perform in the course of writing songs. Just as we will be very specific in describing various containers for your work, we will suggest specific protocols and activities to use those resources effectively.

3. **Principles and Guidelines**. Throughout the book, I offer underlying principles for the practices described, and guidelines for getting the most value out of those practices.

CONCLUDING THOUGHTS

As we prepare to begin our journey through the creative workflow of the song, I would like to touch briefly on two final aspects of your songwriting practice that I wish to honor and acknowledge, but will not address in detail in this book.

Honor the Muse

Underlying the work of songwriting is a deep well of techniques and practices that have to do with general creativity and inspiration. Just as details about song craft are mostly beyond our scope in this book, I'll assume you will draw on these broader techniques and learn about them as necessary. If you are so stuck that your work isn't flowing at all, your problem probably isn't managing creative workflow, it's getting creatively unstuck. Let's call this a plumbing problem—here, I'm just helping you direct the water once it comes out of the faucet.

I do believe most serious songwriters ground their work in some underlying spiritual practice (whether explicit or implicit), and find their own ways to honor the creative spirit—the Muse. With respect, I will leave that part of your journey up to you.

Feed the Poor

This leads directly back to Steve Leslie's third maxim. In this book, I won't lecture you about how to be a good person, whatever that means to you. The point of Steve's maxim, I think, is to remind us that to become great songwriters, to write songs great in soul as well as craft, we should aspire to write songs about things greater than ourselves. At the same time, no matter how noble the content of our songs, we remain both songwriters and regular folks—citizens of our respective and multiple communities.

Your songwriting work will definitely feel different if and when you start writing beyond yourself. This doesn't mean you must sit down immediately and write a song called "Feed the Poor." But it should encourage you to think about the connections between your songwriting, your creative work in general, and your desired positive effect in the world. I do believe the practices we explore together in this book will help you frame these questions. Again, though, I will leave this work up to you.

Do the Housekeeping

This final picture shows the central role of creative workflow management, the focus of this book, in your overall songwriting practice. What I've called the housekeeping—perhaps a better word is *songkeeping!*—integrates craft, business focus, project and task management, and your values, ethics, and purpose as a songwriter.

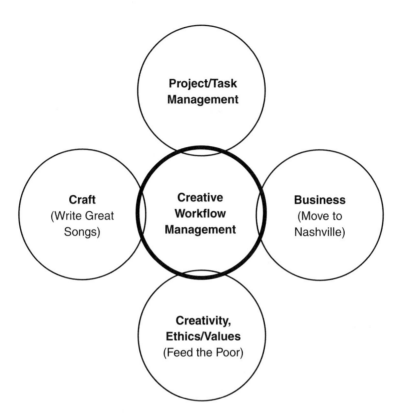

FIG. 1.4. The Central Role of Creative Workflow Management

Creative workflow management practices are not a magic formula that replaces work on craft: what you need to know to write a great song, or a hit song (not always the same thing). Nor are they a sure-fire way to succeed at the *business* of songwriting: to get that famous artist or producer to listen to your song, or to become a viral Web sensation. They are just the work you need to do, while you generate all those drafts and get better at the craft, while you dance through the dizziness and tend to the business.

These may strike you as niggling little details. But there are devils in these details—devils who may come to taunt and frustrate you with impish glee if you don't tend to them and give them their due. Happily, there are angels in these details too—angels who will come to inspire, aid, and guide you. If you do the work.

CHAPTER 2

Managing Your Creative Workflow

"That which we can speak of we can speak of clearly. The rest we should pass over in silence."

—Ludwig Wittgenstein

CHALLENGES IN MANAGING CREATIVE WORKFLOW

I've claimed that there are aspects of the creative work of writing songs that can't be handled in the same ways as conventional business tasks and projects. Before introducing key concepts we will need for effective approaches to managing creative workflow, it will help to look at some distinctive aspects of that workflow, and distinctive challenges these aspects present.

Uncertainty and Indeterminacy

One fundamental aspect of the songwriting endeavor that makes it very hard to manage is its inherent indeterminacy and uncertainty: our lack of direct control, as songwriters, over both ends of the "arc" between inspirations and opportunities. We deal with unpredictability, both in how we initially capture ideas for songs, and in those songs' ultimate placements in the marketplace. Luckily, in the middle things are—also unpredictable.

- *Inspirations.* Songwriters gathering inspirations are, in a sense, acting like radio receivers scanning the airwaves. You can't actually *decide* to find a song seed; rather, it often feels as if it found you. Whether they come from inner sources— stuff that "pops into your head"—or fragments of material captured from the external world, we experience ideas and inspirations not as products of our own volition, but as *arriving, coming to us,* at intermittent times not fully under our control. At certain periods, in hyper-stimulated states of receptivity, ideas may pour in as a torrent; at other times, they may slow to a trickle, or—in writer's block—appear to dry up altogether. (A song seed–catching discipline, by the way, is a powerful antidote for writer's block for this very reason.) Since inspirations may arrive unpredictably, and not in dedicated settings, we must develop practices to *regularly* catch them, with a fairly good yield, while not letting that activity completely disrupt our daily life rhythms.

- *Opportunities.* At the other end of the process, we are constantly working to get those songs—our darlings (well, those we haven't killed)—out into the world. Here we also deal with uncertainty at many levels: When will opportunities arise? Will our work be accepted, or successful? It's true that, just as we can "prospect" for song ideas, we can proactively seek out opportunities—essentially in a *sales* or *marketing* function, except that each song is a different product with a potentially different market. Ultimately, though, this business end of songwriting—like inspirations—is *also* out of our direct control: opportunities *arrive,* and we must decide whether to pursue them.

Messiness

In the middle ground—the work of transforming seeds and inspirations into songs—we deal yet again with a high degree of uncertainty and indeterminacy. The process is inherently subjective, non-linear, iterative, and emergent—in a word, *messy.* (That's why we love it, by the way.)

Part of what makes it messy is our need to save a lot of ancillary material, of different kinds. Music business procedures can tell us much about how to manage finished songs as intellectual property, via copyright, registering with a performing rights organization (PRO), etc. But the completed songs in a songwriter's catalog are just the tip of a big iceberg. We generate a lot of creative material in the *process* of writing songs. The nature of songwriting and the ways songwriters work present some thorny problems around this creative material: basically, we make a lot of mess. We have to.

As a point of comparison, most performers don't regularly record every practice session or rehearsal, unless they intend to use the recording to address learning goals (as an athlete might use video to perfect a certain stroke, swing, or pole-vault).

Songwriters aren't in the same situation. They're not practicing something that already exists; they're *making stuff up*. So they *do* need to keep track of their "practice sessions." After all, that is where their "stuff" comes from. (You know you're making stuff up when what you just played or sang may be the first—and possibly last—time you played or sang it!)

Twyla Tharp, in her excellent book *The Creative Habit* (Simon & Schuster, 2006), describes how she depends on videotaping her working sessions as a choreographer. She has found she can't simultaneously cultivate the fluidity and spontaneity of movement she needs when choreographing (or "dancing to choreograph") with the memory, evaluation, comparison, and related mental processes needed to review, select, edit, rearrange, and reshape that material for the final composition. The same is true of composers—and certainly songwriters—though we may need only an audio and not a video record.

In writing songs, we potentially generate a mountain of creative material, and must hang onto it at least long enough to sift through it and somehow turn it into something. How much? Every songwriter is constantly negotiating this tension. Hang on to *everything*, and risk burying the important nuggets of gold in a heap of archived material that may take as long to wade through as the original session? Or make preemptive guesses as to what will be worth preserving, and risk losing that spontaneous moment of creation you won't quite recapture, even moments later? Usually, we're so happy to have finished a song that we leave material dangling and scattered, in varied states of completion, quality, and entanglement with co-writers. So it stays around—unless we need it, when it often turns out we threw it away.

Abundance

How much of this stuff *do* we really need? Often in songwriting, we are highly *divergent* at the start, and become *convergent* only later, in revising the song. So it is typical, and in fact beneficial, to your craft to generate a lot of draft material, relative to the extent of the final work.

Thus, for songwriters, the uncertainty of inspirations and opportunities is combined with a quintessential over-abundance. Inevitably—in fact, ideally—you will gather many more seeds and inspirations than you can possibly turn into songs. You will also generate many drafts for each finished song, write many songs that you never demo, and demo songs that are never recorded. In fact, I advise students to expect—aspire—to generate from two to *ten* times more material in pre-writing and drafting than there is room for in the song. I call this the "abundance principle."

Of course, much of this stuff will be . . . what's the technical term I'm looking for? Ah yes! "Crap." In fact, if it isn't, that may itself be evidence that your flow-based generative work is too carefully controlled and calculated, your demand for only pleasing results imposing too tight a filter. Yet, if you consider it *all* crap unless something "sticks in your head," you impose too ruthlessly Darwinian a judgment on your work. If you only honor what sticks in your head after three hours of experimentation, why capture anything at all?

Can we turn to technology to help solve this problem? While it can help in some ways, in other ways technology can actually contribute to or exacerbate the problem—or create new problems. Technology gives us the illusion that saving material is cost-free. It doesn't inherently help us manage what we save; on the contrary, it makes it too easy to save *too much*. If you make use of technology's capabilities for saving versions, annotating changes, etc., you can very quickly get simply overwhelmed with data.

If you're doing your job right, you are generating *a lot of stuff*. And the more free-spirited, improvisatory, and generative you are, the more creative material you will generate. This means songwriters must wrangle a huge amount of "data"— material unique to their ways of working. This is not a bad thing; but it's certainly hard to manage it all.

Granularity and Multiple Threads

Besides these three Furies—uncertainty, messiness, and abundance—songwriters face the additional challenge of dealing with very *fine-grained* material in their creative work. As an artistic form, songs are relatively small works, more comparable to poems than to novels, or to fiddle tunes rather than symphonies. (It's no coincidence that music videos are shorter than documentary films!) So, our one big endeavor—writing songs— looks not like a succession of projects, but a river of separate currents, or perhaps a cloth woven of many threads: some separate, some splitting or converging, some getting tangled. If this is true of songs themselves as creative works, it is even more true of the small fragmentary bits of material we capture as seeds or starting inspirations—which might be as small as a single word or phrase.

In addition, small and compact though a song may be, its creation may still involve many rounds of change and revision. This can vary from song to song, and from writer to writer. At the same time, a writer might be working concurrently on many songs, in varying stages of completion. Each song is its own effort, yet material might get shifted around or saved for later. Like I said, it's messy.

ELEMENTS OF CREATIVE WORKFLOW

This odd combination of uncertainty, endless bounty, a ruthless Darwinian die-off rate at both ends of the cycle, and a multi-threaded tapestry of individual creative strands, makes managing the creative workflow of songwriting a fairly daunting enterprise. To draw some order out of this chaotic flow, we'll need to define some terms and concepts that will show up in many stages of the process. We can usefully get a handle on two aspects of creative workflow: *activities* we perform to make stuff, and *material*, the stuff we make.

Activities

Embedded in our intellectual property laws is the definition of a compositional work as a creative expression *embodied* in some *fixed form*: written on a page, recorded on audio or video, etc.

Defining a composition in this way—or to be precise, a composition protectable via copyright law—does not devalue less tangible kinds of creative time and activity that might not produce such an embodied expression. Some creative activity happens only in our minds, as when we stare out the window or wake from a dream. Or we might audibly produce creative sounds but in an only ephemeral way, humming a new tune while walking down the street or improvising on the guitar for a charmed hour. For songwriters, such patient time spent in creative play is essential for developing craft. Without that staring-out-the-window time, that noodling-on-your-guitar time, the work wouldn't happen. The songs wouldn't come.

But unless and until we capture that expression, we are entirely dependent on *memory*. Though we might have begun what could become a timeless song, if we forget it, it's gone. Even if we do remember it later, we're back in the same boat: until we *capture* it in some form, it's as ephemeral as our thoughts. We have to catch even timeless songs in time.

So, in talking about creative workflow in songwriting, the activities we will consider are those involved with producing, or transforming, embodied materials—*work products.* As we'll see throughout the book, however, many activities needed to sustain a songwriting practice won't look like songwriting directly. Some activities are even clerical, or custodial: sorting through lists, transcribing, recopying drafts, etc.

Work Products

The end products of songwriting are the materials we use to embody and document the song in its finished form: lyric sheets, chord and lead sheets, audio tracks with accompanying beats. But songwriting also involves all kinds of intermediate materials or *work products*: not directly part of the song, but that we create in order to get the song written. This is sometimes called "pre-writing" material, but it can be generated at any point in the process, interleaved with bits of the song itself. Such material might include:

- lists of fragmentary notes for song ideas—what I call *song seeds*
- external source material such as Web links, documents, photographs, and newspaper articles
- textual material such as written notes, free writing, object writing, rhyme worksheets, crossed-out drafts, and numerous revisions

- chord charts, notated melodies, or other formal or informal musical notation
- audio recordings, from fragments of seed ideas hummed into our phone, to song sketches, rough demos, or final recordings of finished songs

Work products can also include materials we generate in order to reflect on the creative work itself, either to carry forward to new songs or to improve our craft: notes and reflections, logs and journal entries, session debriefs, lists of favorite songs, or hackneyed phrases to avoid.

A songwriter's *creative workflow* is this intricate and extended dance of activities, work products, and final products or works, particular to the creative work of songwriting.

Visualizing Creative Workflow

The diagram "key" shown in figure 2.1 is a guide to conventions for more detailed workflow diagrams that appear in later chapters. Boxes represent work products of various kinds: physical or digital, text or audio, etc. A series of stacked boxes represent successive versions or iterations. Circles represent activities. Arrows represent creative material worked with in songwriting activities, that flow into and out of work products.

In general, later stages of a song's life cycle are reflected by movement *downward* in the picture. (Given the non-linear and iterative nature of songwriting, though, material will often loop back and swirl around!) Depicting work products and activities toward the left is intended to suggest the "inspirational" side of workflow, or reflective activities such as logs. Depicting work products and activities toward the right indicates more outward-facing opportunities and final products. These directional cues are meant to be only suggestive.

You may find it helpful to redraw the workflow of each stage of the process as *you* understand it, in a way that makes intuitive visual sense for you. You might try, *before* working through the rest of the book, drawing a picture of your current songwriting workflow as you imagine it. As you work through the book, decide what changes or refinements you'd like to experiment with. Draw *that* as a picture, and use the visualization to help you stay on course with your new practices.

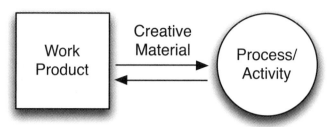

FIG. 2.1. Workflow Diagrams: Key to Conventions

BOUNDARIES AND CONTAINERS

We've characterized creative workflow as an interplay of activities and work products. In order to know *how* to structure these flows, we can take a complementary view: looking at various *boundaries* inherent to songwriting as a creative process, and how different activities and work products can act as *containers* that help us establish and maintain those boundaries.

Creative work is inherently hard to manage because it can feel formless, arbitrary, and free-flowing to a fault or a difficulty. One starting point is establishing *boundaries* around and within that work. The goal is not to kill your creativity, or to overly regiment your work's natural and organic rhythms, but to impose just enough order and constraint to help you manage that work and those rhythms more effectively—not to destroy, but to discipline.

We establish and maintain boundaries in creative practice with tools I will call—in the most generic sense—*containers.* I use this purposely vague term because we can implement a container in widely varied forms or media: journals, notebooks, folders on computers, digital artifacts within apps, etc. To maintain a boundary effectively, a container needs to be both embodied in specific kinds of work products and supported by specific activities and practices—to put material of only a certain kind in that container, or to examine what's in the container at regular intervals. We also create containers, in a sense, for *activities* themselves: dedicated *times* and *places* for doing certain kinds of creative work. This can include routines, appointments, rituals, favorite writing spots, etc.

Boundaries Around Our Songwriting

One all-important boundary is the one we establish around our songwriting as a whole. In *Songwriting Strategies*, I used the metaphor of the Songwriter's Compass to portray songwriting as a kind of transmutation—as if casting a *magic circle* around the song. The World—the source of any kind of content for our songs—lies outside this circle. In writing a song, we carry content, an inspiration gleaned from the World—a scrap of conversation, a story, a theme, a sound—across this mysterious boundary. As we move it across the boundary, we transform it into material of one or more core facets (rhythm, lyric, melody, harmony). Now it's become a a fragment of "song stuff": language set as a lyric-to-be, a melody, a chord progression, or a rhythmic pattern to become lyric, melody, or chords.[1]

Anything you do to reinforce this sense of a boundary around your creative work will indeed help you feel more like a songwriter: having designated lists where you record song seeds, not intermixed with laundry lists and phone numbers; keeping a songwriting journal, rather than just stray papers or pages in your personal diary; having a special spot in the house where you go to write songs. A boundary focuses energy, consecrating and uniting what it holds within.

The mere act of designating a *place* to put a particular kind of creative material changes your engagement with that material. Even if you get confused, the questions you begin to ask about what belongs or doesn't belong there deepen the creative work itself.

Boundaries Within Creative Workflow

Besides boundaries around our songwriting work as a whole, we need to maintain key boundaries within the creative workflow itself. What kinds of boundaries are critical to the nature of songwriting as creative work? We can consider this is in terms of the journalist's standard set of questions: *Who? What? When? Where? Why?* and *How?* Here are a few examples in each of these categories of tools and techniques we'll describe in more detail in the chapters to come.

---

1. I borrowed the imagery of the compass from sources like Wiccan traditions, where a ritual begins by inviting in participants, casting a circle, then invoking spirits of elemental forces to help with the work at hand, be it healing, action, or simple community and celebration. It is indeed a magical moment when you hear an idea, a phrase, suddenly start to "sing" in this way.

Who?

As a songwriter, an important *who* boundary question involves the negotiation between your personal, biographical self and your "songwriter self." Each writer and artist defines and manages this boundary in different ways. For example, we can distinguish two broadly contrasting ways of conceiving songwriting as an art form—or, if you will, as literary genre. Some writers treat their songs as extensions of their journal: an art of *memoir*. Others are clear about, and delight in, their songs creating a fictional world, wherein the Singer sings to a Sung-To about things Sung About in that world.

While true for any creative art, this boundary is particularly permeable and fuzzy given the nature of songwriting. Songwriters, for example, often reshape ordinary, conversational speech, not merely transcribing but musicalizing it. That means some of the time we spend as songwriters is necessarily interwoven with time spent interacting in daily life.

How you conceive of the boundary between your personal and your writing selves will be reflected in many decisions about how to organize your creative material and workflow. For example, whether you keep separate lists of seeds or mix them in with lists of daily chores and tasks, or whether you maintain a song journal separate from your personal diary might seem like mundane or purely practical choices, but reflect more quintessential decisions about these boundaries. Therefore, they can have surprisingly powerful effects on your songwriting as a whole.

Another *who* boundary concerns the *provenance* of material we collect as starting inspirations for songs. You handle material differently depending on whether *you* generated it (a *seed*), or it is a link or reference to outside material (a *source*). Your system of containers will need to distinguish *stuff you made up* from *resources from others to utilize in your creative work*. (We'll explore this further in the next chapter, distinguishing between your *seed notebook* and *commonplace book*.)

An additional *who* boundary, ever more integral to contemporary songwriting practice, involves co-writing and collaboration. This work produces all kinds of materials of shared provenance and potential ownership. Knowing what material is your solo work, versus what is entangled (hopefully happily) in your collaborative work with others, is essential housekeeping. This will be the focus of much of the discussion in chapter 7.

These three *who* boundary questions, among others (my *personal* or my *songwriting* material? *my* material or *someone else's? solo* or *co-written* material—or material of my co-writers?!) can be interwoven in subtle ways, and at times present us with ambiguous gray areas. They must be negotiated nonetheless.

What?

Boundary questions around *what* concern the types of creative material you are managing. This can include distinctions between song seeds, drafts, iterative versions, finished "fair copy" versions, etc., as well as varied types of creative material—lyrics, melodies, chords, beats, found sounds, etc. Each of these may require different kinds of handling, from capture and notation to archiving. The key is to come up with the distinctions and categories that will help you do your work in the most effective way. This will be much of our focus in chapters 3, 4, 5, and 6.

When, Where, How?

Other important boundaries involve *when* and *where* you do songwriting work. Some writers establish particular times of day for working on songs. I find early morning (often before dawn) is my magic time. I love being up before dawn, when all the world is asleep, and with the illusion of having infinite time to work (sadly an illusion; 8:00 A.M. has this pesky habit of rolling around). Some like to set aside particular days for working on songs. Interwoven with time are space and place (as Einstein discovered, though not about songwriting). Perhaps for you, your couch, your porch, or the neighborhood café is the right place to write.

In addition to where (in the real world) you do your work, when it comes to work products you create, there's another *where*: where do you *write it down*, or record it in some other fixed form? And of course, there's the *how*. How do you arrange notebooks, file folders on your computer, lists on your phone? (Does it matter? And how!)

Why?

Last but not least, the question of *why* you write songs—how your songwriting connects to your other professional, artistic, and life roles—provides a central reference point to help you set priorities and focus efforts in every aspect of your workflow. As I mentioned earlier, your system for creative workflow doesn't solve all your problems of task management, work, and business organization. But it is, in a sense, the delivery system by which you get creative output into *actionable order*: to get songs written for your next album, to pitch songs to your chosen market, to write songs for placements—or to write the songs that accord with your mission, to help advance causes and outcomes in the world you care most about. Given the reality of constantly dealing with too many inspirations and too many opportunities, your answer to *why* you are writing songs establishes an all-important boundary. It's how you know when to say yes, and when to say no.

All these questions can be seen as maintaining boundaries through practices involving different kinds of containers—be they lists, notebooks, or scheduled writing sessions. These habits and conventions will shape the pace, quality, and tenor of your work.

ESTABLISHING NEW WORKFLOW PRACTICES

In the remainder of this book, we will tour through the entire "life cycle" of creating songs: from initial inspirations, through drafts and versions, critiques and revisions, to co-writing, demo recording, and catalog management. At each stage and transition between stages, our emphasis will be on managing the workflow of creative materials and activities. Some work products, like song seed notebooks, are containers that will help you negotiate the subtle interplay between the desiderata of everyday life and your creative work as a songwriter; some exist within the flow of the creative work itself, to help you establish order in the essential fluidity of that work; and some help in the "staging" of that creative output—to get those songs out into the world. At each point, you will need to design and shape your own workflow: a kind of choreography or architecture that supports the artistic work of your songwriting—the real *why* in all of this.

CHAPTER 3

Managing Seed and Source Material

SEEDS AND SOURCES

A song often begins with a single, discrete point of inspiration. I have found the term *song seeds* a useful and evocative metaphor for these kinds of inspirations. In my classes, workshops, and my book *Songwriting Strategies*, I describe the process of gathering these kernels of inspirations for songs as "song seed catching." When I started teaching seed-catching skills, I discovered that many writers I encountered were already regularly catching seeds, though they often didn't ascribe much importance to the activity, sometimes even feeling a bit sheepish about it. And at first, I felt almost sheepish as well: as if I'd done little else but give a name to a practice songwriters were already employing. But as I formalized the notion of song seeds, I gradually began to articulate a more formal discipline of seed catching as an intentional practice. In addition, as I listened to writers' experiences and difficulties, I realized certain supporting tools were critical for a song seed practice to be truly effective.

One summer, I led some songwriting workshops at the idyllic Miles of Music camp, on beautiful Three Mile Island (not *that* Three Mile Island!) on Lake Winnipesaukee. On our first day, a songwriter told the group, "I am always catching song scraps and ideas, but don't know what to do with them. They wind up as sticky notes around the edge of my mirror, scribbles on napkins, etc."

Instead of empowering her, her ways of catching seeds—or rather, handling the seeds she caught—were making her anxious and frustrated. She had the initial seed-catching *activity* down, but not the housekeeping—the follow-up. In response, I pulled from my pocket a little red Moleskine 2" x 3" pocket notebook, held it aloft conspicuously for all to see, and talked about how empowering it could be to simply have a *place* to collect one's seeds. That week, the Little Red Notebook became a kind of mascot for all the songwriters.

Without the right tools and practices in place, getting better at catching seeds can even make your creative workflow management problem *worse*, as you catch more and more seeds without knowing how to handle them. This may be partly a problem of craft, but often it is more about managing workflow in a way that energizes creative responses.

To be useful, a song seed process must help you maintain certain key boundaries. You need ways to:

- Sift song seeds from everyday material not related to songs.
- Differentiate original seeds from various kinds of outside source material.
- Separate the fragmentary "snapshot" the seed represents from material you generate as you "work" (develop and expand) the seed.

This is all, so to speak, the "data wrangling" part of managing your seeds. You also need to manage the creative activities around engaging with your seeds. For example, it is liberating when you break the thread of urgency and compulsion between capturing a seed and working on it. Your creative workflow becomes far more manageable, especially in relation to daily life; you're less likely to be sideswiped by the Muse demanding hours of your time—right now!—when you really need to get your taxes done. Yet maintaining your song seed list without a supporting practice that assures you *will* dip into those seeds on a regular basis can backfire, becoming a kind of collusion with avoidance. (I know this all too well. I was willing to keep my own song seed lists for many years without such supporting practices, and paid a price for it.)

Of course, you can capture initial creative expressions in many other ways than the specific song seed–catching practices I like to describe. You can sit on the porch noodling on your guitar until you stumble onto an idea, go into a studio to record long improvisatory jams, or fill journal pages in the morning. But there are reasons I put song seed practices front and center. Most other ways of generating inspirational material embody it in forms that are relatively easy to differentiate *as* creative material. We will describe ways to manage those kinds of materials in chapter 5, when we talk about song sketches, drafts, and versions. But seeds, as a specific type and texture of creative material, present distinctive challenges due to their highly fragmentary nature and the necessity of catching them in the midst of everyday activities. That makes for some tricky workflow management tasks.

Furthermore, working efficiently with the materials generated by more flow-based methods often involves listening back through those materials and—surprise!—catching seeds again, this time from your own work. In the same way, song seeds— peripheral creative materials, as it were—arise in the midst of co-writing and song revision. At the same time, that initial seed-catching work provides the most value as you access the material later in songwriting. We make use of both the seed material itself and of seed-catching practices throughout the entire creative life cycle of songwriting.

WORK PRODUCTS FOR MANAGING SEEDS

Seeds come in different *facets*: lyric ideas, concepts for songs (also captured by textual phrases that are less likely destined to become actual lyrics), melodies, chord progressions, riffs, beats, etc. A primary challenge in seed catching is finding ways to effectively capture—transcribe, notate, record, etc.— varied types of creative material. The biggest difference is the media used: *writing* something down, or *recording* it in audio, audiovisual, or even visual form (e.g., screenshots and photos). Lyrical material and concepts can be recorded either way; musical material can be notated in various forms, but that presents challenges depending on the type of material, and on your notation skills and familiarity with both informal and formal notation.

Workflow Challenges in Seed Catching

Before discussing specific tools, containers, and procedures for capturing and managing seeds, let's review the nature of song seeds and the workflow challenges they present:

- We want to be ready to catch seeds at times when we are not necessarily prepared to do focused creative work. The tools we use to capture seeds must coexist with our everyday activities as much as possible.

- At the same time, we need to capture seeds in ways that clearly set them aside from other workaday material, so we can find and work with them later.

- Seeds are fragmentary. In fact, with increasing skill in seed catching, you write less, not more. We need ways to capture seeds that lend themselves to large numbers of very small bits of content. For example, if we write seeds in one large document, at some point we will need to break that document up into smaller pieces that we can reorder, sift, and rearrange.

- Seeds tend to be unfamiliar, novel material not heard before. So they are easy to forget, but also easy to "kinda sorta" remember. Little quirky details can get rubbed away, approximated, or eroded by imperfect recall— details that may be essential to what made the seed compelling. Our seed-catching tools and techniques must be readily available at short notice and for short bursts of transcription. They must provide ways to catch subtle details, but just the details we care about. You don't have time to produce precise staff notation of the microtonal bends and rhythmic nuances of that little tune bouncing around in your head. But you must have a notation format (and the skills to use it) sufficient to catch anything distinctive about the seed. You can make a recording, but eventually, you need to listen back to that recording and transcribe it, or recreate it on your instrument.

Seed-Catching Notebook

As discussed, songwriters gather seeds in an endless variety of ways and places. But while napkin jottings have a romantic appeal, and someday may be worth who-knows-how-much on eBay or to your future biographers, there is great procedural efficiency as well as psychological potency in designating an honored container—a *talisman*, as it were—for your seeds.

I like to use a physical artifact for catching song seeds: a small paper *seed notebook*. (I use the term "log" or "logbook" for more chronological records, as in a "captain's log.") You'll want to experiment with different sizes, designs, formats, colors, etc. There's no one right answer—not only because songwriters are individuals, but also because there are inherent tradeoffs. But what you choose matters, as you will learn by trying out varied formats, noting and reflecting on their different effects. Here are key aspects to consider in terms of designing your seed-catching apparatus:

Size

Song seeds come to us during everyday activities, out of peripheral attention. Your notebook should be small enough to be easy to carry with you at almost all times. But how small is small? There's no one right answer, but small things make a big difference. I found that using a smaller 2x3 inch, versus 3x5 inch, notebook changed my practice significantly: both the length (or granularity) of seeds I captured, and how I clustered them. This impact of physical limitations of the notebook is analogous to the power of time constraints in writing exercises such as object writing. Diving deep into describing an apple, knowing you have just three minutes, engages improvisational energy and rapid immersion skills. Similarly, jotting seeds on small pages reminds you to capture just the seed—and fast!

With a smaller notebook, you'll also be more comfortable writing just one seed on a page—maybe even using just one side of each page, so you can later tear pages out and sort them into piles. Small pages thus encourage you to write down smaller seeds, not entire song drafts. On the other hand, you might start trying to crowd whole song lyrics onto that tiny page, out of a perverse desire to defeat the medium. With a slightly larger page size, you will be more tempted to make a page a *list* of seeds, and later find yourself processing lists of lists. Or you may start to make seeds more the length of couplets or verses rather than individual lines, out of an instinctive desire to fill the whole page. Whatever format you use, observe its effects on your creative practice. Be attentive to when you start to use workarounds or subvert the inherent discipline that a particular format encourages.

Physical vs. Digital

By physical, I mean "hard copy"—paper with a cover. I can't imagine what new digital, skin temperature–controlled neurally wired version of song seed–catching apps may eventually be at (or inlaid into) our fingertips. But as a lonely voice crying out from the Gutenberg-to-post-McLuhan phase of human notational history, I'd like to put in a plea for the Power of Paper. (I do sometimes call my notebook my "old-time Palm Pilot"— now there's a dated technology reference!)

I remember being greeted at a Berklee commencement by a student from several years prior. He proudly pulled a dog-eared seed notebook from his hip pocket and said he'd been practicing seed catching faithfully, ever since taking my class. It had become a central part of his creative practice, and a source of many of his strongest songs. It was a satisfying moment for me, knowing I'd successfully corrupted at least one young, impressionable mind! And I confess that the very dog-eared wornness of the notebook was part of the satisfaction I felt.

My affection for physical seed notebooks may be in part a generational predilection, or a matter of personal style and taste. But I also believe that there are subtle, yet significant, differences in the experiential effects of physical activities of transcription into different media. Artist, author, and creative philosopher Linda Barry has written eloquently about the creative impact of the visual and tactile gestures required for writing by hand. While we will return to these questions in chapter 5, when we discuss song journals and drafts, they have an impact even in the first stages of capturing ideas and seeds.

I recommend that you inquire into, experiment with, and reflect on how *your* creative process changes when you capture a seed, or write a draft of lyrics, by hand versus on a computer or mobile device. Spend some time consistently using one medium and protocol, then another, and then compare the results.

Here's an instance where I've done my own homework! Over a period of several years, I gradually migrated my own seed-catching activity mostly to audio memos and text captured via a notes app on my smartphone and laptop. Occasionally, I'd go back to paper notebooks, and at times I had both systems in place. The results were intriguing, and certainly not a black-and-white choice. Certain kinds of capturing were made easier, others more difficult.

One surprising discovery had to do with the effects of difficulties in each medium. Because I am older and didn't grow up with hand-held technology, I lack what I like to call the "text-hensile thumbs" of my younger student friends. So, especially at first, I would make lots of mistakes and typos catching seeds on my phone. Occasionally, these mistakes would be unintentionally revealing and even of creative interest. More significantly, I found that the very struggle to capture ideas in this way shifted the pace and flow of my creative work. The interruptions could be frustrating, or also curiously energizing. Ironically, for younger songwriters with a different relationship to technology, capturing material with pen on paper might present similar challenges.

One partial explanation for this effect might lie in the dynamic of "effortful encoding": the theory that when we must work a little harder to write something down, we will remember it better. While this concept has emerged in research done mostly in the context of retention of received information in educational settings, it is interesting to speculate how this dynamic might also affect the *generation* of content in creative work.

Since each writer is different, explore for yourself how the medium of capture can shape the form and even the quality of your inspirations. Becoming more aware of the subtle influences of the medium on the message is, in the end, the most important lesson.

Ultimately, I have found I use both formats in tandem, both for practical reasons and perhaps because of the experiential qualities of each. I catch many seeds while working on the computer, but many when neither computer nor phone is handy, or would be disruptive. I want my seed-catching containers to be as seamlessly embedded as possible into each immediate work context where I'm likely to engage in peripheral seed-catching activity. (For me, at least, that means any and all of them!)

Recording Devices

Some types of seeds are better caught on a digital device. For capturing musical seeds—rhythms, melodies, chord progressions, or sounds—an audio recording device is a natural tool to use, and one now ubiquitously available with the advent of handheld computer technology. (We'll discuss audio recordings of musical seeds later in this chapter.) It is also sometimes more convenient, or more effective, to capture even verbal seed material via recording. This allows you to capture aspects of pace and rhythmic setting along with the language itself. Newer voice transcription technologies also blur these distinctions, as you can use voice input with text-based transcription.

Song Seeds: Workflow Design

Managing workflow involves setting up both the containers or work products you need—documents, lists, books, etc.—and the supporting practices, habits, and disciplines to make those work products *work* for you. How you work with song seeds, and especially with your song seed notebooks, offers a useful "deep dive" example of the often-subtle principles and issues that arise in designing and maintaining your creative workflow. We need to keep seed material separate from everyday work materials, but also separate from later creative drafts. Two brief anecdotes help illustrate this.

At the Miles of Music workshop described earlier, my dramatic Raising of the Red Notebook moment apparently made an impression on Nora, a talented eleven-year-old banjo player and budding songwriter who had faithfully attended every (early!) morning session. Later, I had gone on to explain how I number my song journals (as will be discussed in chapter 5). At lunch that day, song seeds were flying around the dining hall table. I had dutifully pulled out my red notebook, when Nora asked, with a wise-beyond-her-years sober intensity, "What number is *that* one?" I explained that I do *not* number my song seed notebooks the way I number my journals. "Why not?" she asked. For a moment, I felt abashed—as if caught out. Then I stopped to reflect: why *do* I treat my seed notebooks as a different "archival category" than my permanent song journals?

The answer to that innocent question turned out to involve some deep principles of container design for managing creative workflow. My song seed notebooks are important containers, compared to jotting seeds on random scraps of paper. But they are also *ephemeral* containers—because, the way I use them, they contain other material *besides* song seeds. That decision has implications for the way I process material in those notebooks later on.

More recently, working with Talia, a Berklee student songwriter, in the one-on-one directed study sessions songwriting majors take in their later semesters, I happened to ask about her song seed–catching practice. "I have lots of seeds," she said, "but I write them down in my song journals, along with all my drafts and versions."

"How do you find them, then?" I asked—this time, not so innocent a question.

My student had made a simple design decision, early on in her practice: to intermix seed catching with her work on drafts of songs. Though this might seem a tiny housekeeping detail, the effective result was a system that made it extremely difficult for her to access her unworked seeds via a coherent and *separate* resource. In fact, after our discussion, she began a sweep through many years of consecutive journals. This "seed rescue" operation turned into an intensive multi-week effort, yielding major creative insights, discoveries and, more important, rediscoveries.

When you set up any sort of container for creative workflow, you are actually making two procedural decisions, reflecting the complementary dynamics of how containers enforce boundaries and shape workflow: by keeping stuff *in*, and by keeping stuff *out*.

- Centripetal energy—A container *gathers* and *focuses* material when you apply the rule: **I will put this type of material *only here*.**

- Centrifugal energy—A container *concentrates* and *filters* material when you apply the rule: **I will put *only this type of material* here.**

These choices determine much about the kind of containers you'll need, and supporting practices around how you'll use them. While, in principle, these decisions are separable and independent, in practice, we often intertwine them without always thinking them through or even being aware of them as decisions. Yet, they dramatically shape the rhythms and quality of our creative workflow.

To illustrate—when I set up a song seed notebook, I make two independent decisions:

- Will I put seeds *only* in this notebook, or here among other places?
- Will I put *only* seeds in this notebook, or seeds and other stuff?

Shall seeds go only here? Consider the implications. I will try not to scrawl seeds on napkins, bookmarks, stickies in my calendar, or on the back of my hand. If I can trust that every time I write down a song seed, I put it in *that* notebook, I will be confident that any song seeds, *if I caught them*, are there in that book. This provides a powerful focus. I now won't have to go sweeping up seeds later from lots of random places. The notebook acquires centripetal energy: seed material is pulled *toward* the notebook. This also encourages me to catch more seeds. The presence of the notebook in my pocket prompts me to remember to catch those seeds.

This protocol requires a seed notebook that is ubiquitous, ever-present. I'll need a book I can carry easily, get to quickly. Otherwise, when I go to catch a seed and my notebook is not handy, I will have to improvise and write the seed on a scrap of paper instead. Or I'll give up writing down the seed. Either way, I've diluted the notebook's magnetic pull. If caught out, sure, I'll use a napkin rather than lose the seed, but I'll want to repair the process, and keep myself honest by transcribing the seed from that napkin to my notebook (or maybe to another seed list).

Note, though, I can maintain this rule and still write *other things* in that notebook: contact information, to-do lists, and so on. Its very handiness of access invites such multiplicity of uses; ubiquity invites multitasking. Once seeds are intermixed with other stuff, I still get the benefit of the focus of the book, but I have diluted its *coherence*. Now, to use the book, I'll need to skim through and *sift out* seeds from other stuff.

In my own practice, I keep a rolling series of physical notebooks where I try to put *all the seeds* I write down, especially in walking-around mode. Inevitably, though, lots of other kinds of material finds its way in there as well. Those notebooks become way stations for a more permanent recording of seeds. When time allows, I transcribe the seeds out of those notebooks, sometimes into end pages of my current song journal, sometimes directly onto my digital Seed Catalogue (see below). As I transcribe each seed, I cross it out in the notebook pages. When I've handled them all, I can gleefully *throw that notebook away*—or at least take it out of my creative workflow. Clearly, it doesn't make sense to number these sorts of notebooks, hanging onto them or archiving them as permanent books, as I would a dedicated songwriting journal.

PAGES I KEEP

I have one exception to this throwaway treatment of my seed notebooks. Every now and then, writing down a seed feels special, in social situations with other creative types. Lately (perhaps because I'm getting older and more sentimental), I have taken to asking those present at the Capturing of the Seed to sign my song seed notebook. I will date and timestamp the page, and note where the seed was captured. "On this day, in the middle of the woods on Three Mile Island . . ." This is a fun community-building ritual that also helps me later remember the context in which the seed was caught and who was there. When processing a notebook with an "artifact page" of this sort, I tear out the page and save it in a loose-leaf archival file.

I have a similar practice with my full songwriting journal, for co-writing sessions. In those cases, though, the pages stay in the journal in their bound order. The journal already is an artifact (and numbered!).

Shall <u>only seeds</u> go here? This is a different question: it determines what I put in the notebook. This rule, if I adopt it, says this notebook is *special*: no laundry lists, friends' addresses, or to-do list items in here. Only seeds in this notebook!

Sustaining this practice takes a different kind of work and care. When I need to write down a reminder for an appointment, I'll need a different place to put it. But if I maintain this practice, the notebook takes on a kind of *centrifugal* power: it pushes away other kinds of material. The result is concentrated, pure. I'd know, as I leaf through this notebook, that *all I see are seeds*. Working with this kind of notebook is a different kind of creative work, and the notebook itself becomes a different kind of artifact—one I'm far more likely to keep on hand permanently.

In theory, you could also combine *both* protocols, for an "all and only" container, i.e., *all* seeds are transcribed in the notebook; and *only* seeds go into that notebook. This would make a highly focused, potent container that you will identify very strongly with the creative work of songwriting. This protocol, in fact, makes pretty good sense—for a *songwriting journal*.

You might think, wouldn't it be cool to have a single, magical, special notebook for really special seeds you catch? But there are inherent problems with this protocol for seeds, given how song seed catching works. For one thing, as much as possible, we want to defer judgment and evaluation when we catch seeds. I don't want to carry an "everyday seeds" and a fancy "really great seeds" notebook around at the same time. The evaluative thinking I'd need to do to decide in which notebook to record a given seed, at the moment I am ready to capture it, is precisely the *wrong* kind of question to ask at that moment.

Another issue is simply the *abundance* of seeds you want to be catching—many more seeds than you'll ever turn into songs! So, if you're doing your job as song seed catcher, you shouldn't have any single song seed notebook for all that long. If it's big and thick, it's not the "carry everywhere" notebook you need. If it's small and thin, you shouldn't have it for more than a month or two. We humans completely replace our skin cells every seven years or so; you should fill a seed notebook every seven weeks or so.

Thus, there are reasons why song seed notebooks tend not be permanent in the same way as the song journals we will discuss in chapter 5. You want to catch seeds in a container that focuses your energy, while reducing the friction of catching seeds. At the same time, you want that container to be loosely coupled with the work spaces and work products where you will do your focused writing work. We might compare this to the ingenious discovery of the sticky note, by researchers who actually had been trying to develop a new, more effective glue. The half-sticky glue that makes sticky notes do all the useful things they do was originally a design "failure"—but one that proved to have ideal qualities to invent an entirely new category of office item. (That said, my whole purpose here is to urge you *not* to use sticky notes for your song seeds!)

Journal End Pages

Song seed notebooks are essential containers for catching seeds "in the wild"—that is, in the midst of everyday activity. But seed catching has a second aspect: paying attention to *peripheral* ideas. In this second sense, seeds can reveal themselves in peripheral aspects of *any* foreground task requiring focused attention—including *in the course of doing creative work itself.* As you work on a song, getting those creative juices flowing puts your brain into a flow state likely to trigger lots of creative ideas. Some will be relevant to the creative task at hand—the song you're working on—and some will be unrelated, perhaps connected by a chain of association that is not necessarily useful within that song.

It's a valuable insight simply to be aware that the creative process works this way—that as you write one song, you're likely to generate unrelated ideas deserving of their own consideration for and as songs. This awareness will help keep your songs more focused. Just as you learn that you don't need to work a seed into a full song at the moment of first capture, you learn to recognize stray ideas generated while working on a song—ideas that don't necessarily belong to *that* song—seeds that blow in while turning other seeds into songs! This may seem an obvious insight; it's often not. As songwriter, co-writer, and teacher, I've heard (and yes, written!) many songs with extraneous great lines stuck in seemingly at random. "What about that line? You don't need it!"

"Yeah, but I *love* that line!" You are more likely to avoid those pitfalls simply by having *another place to put that line* when you are writing the song.

So, you want to catch these seeds. But where? If you keep them in the context of the journal pages for the song, you risk crowding them into the song, or else losing track and never going back to them. Or you can keep your song seed notebook at hand while working on your song in your journal, but that's a little awkward.

I like to support this awareness of moving between focused and peripheral creative moments, while staying with my journal as my main locus of activity. So, I have developed the practice of transcribing some song seeds in the *end pages* of my songwriting journal. I fill in these end pages in *reverse order* as I gather song ideas, while simultaneously working through the main pages of the journal consecutively, front to back (with dated, numbered pages).

If my songwriting journal is handy when a song seed comes to me, I'll write the seed in the end pages rather than reach for my song seed notebook. (Yes, this dilutes—a bit—the centripetal pull of my song seed notebook as my *only* place to write seeds, but not as badly as, say, writing the seed on a scrap of paper!) But the main purpose of seed list pages at the back of my journal is to focus the songwriting work I do at the front of the journal. When I am working on a song and get one of those cascading flurries of "seeds in the midst of working on seeds," I flip to the end pages and add the seed to that list. (We will see other uses for song seeds captured in end pages when we discuss co-writing in chapter 7.)

Location- and Context-Specific Seed Lists

On the same principle as my "end pages" seed lists, it makes sense to maintain seed lists in any other environments where you are doing creative work, to facilitate rapid and seamless shifts between foreground creative tasks and seed catching. As I work on the computer or laptop, I create digital seed lists so that I can open a separate window, capture the seed, and then go back to my main task.

I anticipate that evolving technologies and applications will increasingly facilitate moving between focused and peripheral creative work in seamless ways, with support for immediate backup, unlimited storage, access and synchronization across devices, multimedia data, labels and searchable tags, etc. Effective use of these technologies will, however, still require good workflow management practices and discipline. Consider the nature of your own varied contexts, environments, and media for creative work. Set up ways to catch seeds or other peripheral creative material in each of these contexts—ways as frictionless as possible. Setting up these containers acknowledges the inherent nature of creative work as a rhythmic series of shifts between focused and peripheral attention.

Seeds in Other Media

Song seeds come in many different modes and facets. And for most songwriters, when a musical rather than lyrical idea pops into your mind or under your fingers, the easiest and quickest way to capture it is via an audio recording. Although it is good to develop your skills for notation and transcription, there will always be types of seed material best captured through recording, for transcribing later. There are, of course, good systems for archiving and collecting audio recordings. But there are particular challenges with catching song *seeds* due to their fragmentary nature, the multitude of seeds you'll catch, and the fact that, as initial fragments, you often won't know what to call them—yet!

MULTIMEDIA SEED CAPTURE

Recording need not imply only audio information. For example, if capturing an idea on guitar that involves novel chord shapes discovered through exploration and discovery, it may be difficult to recreate those shapes and voicings strictly through an audio recording. A photo or video recording accompanying the audio can save huge amounts of time and frustration later. You can also use notation—for example, a series of chord diagrams that sketch the shape and progression. Using both in tandem may be the idea, but requires cross-linking the recordings and notation in some way.

The ubiquity of recording tools on mobile devices has made it easier than ever to catch fleeting musical ideas as short audio (and/or video/photo) "snippets." Many writers accumulate hundreds of these digital files of seeds and sketches. Data management tools for many of these devices were often designed for business-oriented text or voice memos, while music-oriented systems may be architected for longer artifacts representing more complete performances. Such systems may be cumbersome for large sets of very short files, especially where descriptions are imprecise rather than formal titles or a controlled-keyword vocabulary.

Dates and Timestamps

While I date entries in songwriting journals, I generally do *not* date individual song seeds written in notebooks (unless it's one of my "signed" seed pages, for archival or just sentimental value). Usually, though, I put a date range at the front of a song seed notebook, more for convenience than as thorough documentation. In a legal sense, song seeds are, almost by definition, *fragments* of an intended later complete work, and thus *not individually protectable by copyright.* It's when I start *working the seed* into at least a rough draft of a song that the date of that creative work becomes important.

Date and time information plays a far more essential role with audio recordings. Most recording technology automatically dates and timestamps recordings. Often, unless you descriptively label or name a file, a date/timestamp may be the effective tag for the file. I frequently depend heavily on this date and time information to find my way back to a particular recording. If you do listen through seed recordings to generate titles or descriptions, make sure you do not lose the time and date metadata.

The most effective way to use such systems for musical seeds is to keep granularity small. This will generate more individual items to keep track of. But when you accumulate many ideas in a running "seeds" audio file, you may lose date and timestamp information, and wind up with a large conglomerate document you need to sift through. Back in the good old days of cassettes and audiotape, you would inevitably have a series of separate recordings on one piece of media. Digital audio files can be much more granular. So, in audio formats, I tend to use a one seed/one file protocol, and I often create separate "snapshot" files when evolving a musical idea, even in a single consecutive session.

Although you won't have the equivalent of your *Little Red Song Seeds* notebook on your audio-capturing device, it is still good to have some convention for a separate area, album, or other container for recordings representing seeds. Try not to intermix these with other people's music, voice memos, etc. It is also useful to try to maintain a distinction between very short snapshot files—seed ideas proper—and long improvisational jams that you record and "mean to go back through and listen to at some point." The problem with this approach is that, to make use of the material, you have to live through almost the same amount of time listening back as you spent creating it in the first place. Try to break up long recorded sessions, or leave markers or "breadcrumbs," so you can get back efficiently to known spots of "seedly promise."

SEEDS CENTRAL: THE MOTHER SHIP

Song seeds represent a kind of pure creative potential. A song seed list is *not* a to-do list, but a *possibilities* list. Since the very act of capturing seeds lifts and separates them from their original context of capture, they are in an important sense *timeless*. A seed captured in your late teens might productively rub shoulders and unite with a seed captured last week (okay, maybe you're *still* in your late teens!). So, in the grand scheme of things, songwriting-wise, the ideal container would be a single, centralized gathering place for *all* your song seeds. Although you will get there only gradually, it helps to designate some list as your starting point for this "mother ship" where you will concatenate and coalesce your various song seed lists. Let's call it "Seeds Central."

Seeds Central is a single container where all song seeds migrate eventually as you process them—at least, seeds that haven't been used for active songs. While you could implement Seeds Central on a paper system, mine is a digital file on my computer. This makes sense, as this will not be a static document, but something you will mess around with a lot, moving seeds and reordering, sorting, and sifting them. In the next section, we will discuss some of the activities by which your seeds will flow from notebooks, possibly via journal end pages or individual lists, into Seeds Central. There are practical reasons why this sifting and consolidation will only happen at certain times, just as you will only access your full Seeds Central "bank" in certain circumstances. (In theory, if you're working on the computer and your Seeds Central is resident there, you could open it directly to add every new seed. In practice, I don't do this. Seeds Central will rapidly become a *large* file; you will want to open it mostly when you have a reason to interact with the seed bank as a whole.

MANAGING SOURCE MATERIAL FOR SONGS

Song seeds are generally fragments of *original* material—that is, something you created: a melody, a chord progression, a new lyric line. But we songwriters also regularly gather materials and resources we did not generate ourselves, but intend to use—directly or indirectly—in songs or in writing songs. We might call these *sources*, to distinguish them from *seeds*.

Distinctions between seeds and sources can be subtle. We're likely to capture the material in similar ways and from similar sources. The notion of song seeds itself acknowledges the layered and interwoven boundaries between what we generate and what we borrow (or steal). Though our modern culture (and legal system) tends to apply overly simplistic notions of what "wholly original" means, songwriting is as much about transformation as it is about creation from scratch. Songwriters are like magpies, pilfering ideas and bits of language, to varying degrees of "verbatim-ity," from everywhere and everyone: media sources (books, television, social media), casual conversations with friends, things overheard in coffeehouses, etc.

Provenance

A primary distinction between ways of handling seeds versus sources arises when you decide whether to retain information about the provenance of material you intend to work with creatively, at the time you first capture or record it.

Rather than flail for a philosophically grounded bright-line distinction, I suggest you differentiate between what you treat as seed versus source in terms of a few key criteria:

- for legal, contractual, or ethical reasons
- because a possible co-writing or collaborative relationship might be created
- to make the final song more compelling to the listener, or more marketable
- to enrich your own reflection on your creative process, or for a "making of" narrative.

There are particular points of songwriting etiquette and ethics to observe in interactions with other creative artists. I never intentionally grab a song seed from a fellow songwriter, even in casual conversation or from social media; instead, I generally toss it back to them, then perhaps may offer to co-write it with them. However, passing quips from folks I call "civilians" are fair game!

When content you are adapting is from a different media source, lines can get blurrier. I often take text from a poem, newspaper article, or social media post and transform it into material for song lyrics. My rule of thumb: if I draw more than a single isolated phrase from one source, my creative relationship and obligation to record that source changes. On occasion, I have found a piece of writing so compelling, filled with song-worthy phrases and images, that I have drawn a significant portion of a song from that one source. One example is my song "Sweet Outrage," written from a newspaper article about skinheads causing trouble in the town of Billings, Montana. In that case, I contacted the reporter and offered co-writer credit on the song. Though he declined, he was delighted his material had turned into a song.

In addition to good housekeeping around material that may be borderline in status, there is also virtue in establishing creative practices around working specifically with source material. Engaging with this material is as essential to your creative work as expressing yourself in new work—breathing in versus breathing out. You will inevitably hit dry spells in the rhythms of your creative work. One way to more smoothly navigate those fluctuating currents is to build in time to listen as well as sing, to take it in as well as put it out there. In addition, as described by writers such as Austin Kleon, the artistic environment of the new "networked creative" involves a degree of curatorship and collaboration intermixed with individual creative work. Attending to (and attending), reviewing, and linking in various ways to work of related artists in your genre, scene, and community is integral to your professional work as a songwriter.

Florilegia and Commonplace Books

Alongside your ever-growing collection of song seeds and your published catalog of finished songs, you can envision your gathering of source materials from others as a related, evolving work. In viewing it this way, you are participating in an ancient tradition. In the Middle Ages, scholars created compilations of quotations and extracts from larger works called *florilegia* (from the Latin *flos* [flower] and *legere* [to gather])—literally, a gathering of flowers, or select extracts from a larger work. In later centuries in the Western European cultural tradition, scholars and "people of letters" created *commonplace books.* Clearly distinguished at the time from chronological personal diaries or travel journals, these were compilations of favorite passages from other writers that particularly moved and inspired the compiler, often organized by theme or topic, and evolving over time. Scrapbooking is a more modern version of this sort of compiling and collaging of source material, also with a long history and countless communities of enthusiasts. The older traditions resonate particularly for me as a songwriter, as they were so often assembled by creative artists specifically as source inspirations for their own work.

Today, the traditions of florilegia, commonplace books, and scrapbooking live on digitally via the explosion of social multimedia sites, such as Tumblr, Instagram, and Pinterest. Such sites turn once-passive consumers into micro-curators. Established artists in turn use curatorship for promotion, for their own inspiration, to build community, or to link with related artists.

In a period where there was no mechanical means for copying works, compiling excerpts and quotations required copying texts by hand from the original source. This meant commonplace books became, as it were, one of a kind "artists' books" in their own right. While we have access to instant digital copying for most forms of content today, it is worth considering creating an old-fashioned physical book for yourself along these lines as well. Many musicians and songwriters maintain beautiful, sometimes road-worn journals of hand-copied lyrics. I recall a Berklee clinic where hit songwriter Dean Pitchford described how he had approached learning songwriting, coming from a background as a vocalist and actor. To study the lyrics of great songs, he would copy out the lyrics, *by hand,* into his own notebook. He said he wanted his hand to *feel what it would have felt like* to have written those lyrics!

Songwriters need to manage source materials in different ways, depending on how closely those materials are linked to active songs. You might simply maintain your own archive of "links to interesting stuff" like any other new digital citizen, or keep a separate area for stuff you think *might* provide inspiration for songs in particular, presorting into "Potential Song Material." If and when material serves as inspiration for a particular song, keep track of that linkage; for example, if you maintain a folder for each song, as we will discuss in chapter 9, designate a subfolder for "Source Material."

CHAPTER 4

Supporting Practices for Seed Material

Say that you have been a diligent seed-catcher for some time, and you now have a song seed list with many seeds—at least dozens, perhaps hundreds—of many types and modalities: ideas for songs, titles, hooks and lines, melodies, bits of progressions, grooves, and rhythmic patterns.

But there is a hitch: what if you keep collecting seeds and then *never look at them again*?

This is no hypothetical problem. Many writers collect lots of seeds but can't seem to do anything with them. There are certainly techniques to learn about how to develop different kinds of seed material into songs, but curiously, often the stumbling blocks are less issues of craft or knowledge of songwriting techniques, and more of managing workflow and creative energy. This can involve subtle underlying dynamics, such as plain old fear—seed catching as procrastination made manifest. Or we can get too fond of seed catching itself, for its own sake. Once we lose the anxiety that every seed must quickly become a song, we can relax and enjoy the freedom to "just collect." We discover it's fun to catch seeds—maybe too fun! Getting too good at seed catching can even begin to work against us. Seed catching breaks habitual links between different kinds of creative work. If we previously have counted on the seamlessness of those activities to move us to write, interrupting that mechanism can rob us of that prior motivation.

To better integrate seed catching into our overall songwriting practice, we need to connect our seed lists to creative work in key ways:

1. First, we need to put time into reviewing and consolidating the seed lists themselves.

2. Then, we need a regular practice of going back to the seed lists and writing songs based on those seeds.

3. Finally, we need to understand when and how to make use of the seed lists in other phases of the creative work of songwriting.

CONSOLIDATING SEED LISTS: SORT AND SIFT

As we've discussed, you might legitimately have quite a few places where you are catching song seeds: pocket-sized notebooks, digital files, audio memos, lists at the backs of journals. One background task you will engage in at various times is the work of *consolidating* your seeds, gradually sifting, sorting, trimming, and categorizing them from these various sources into Seeds Central—where good seeds go to wait patiently to be called into service. Although there are many activities involved in this work, I'll summarize it with the catchy phrase *sort and sift*. This work of consolidating your seed lists is mundane but essential housekeeping.

For one thing, you want Seeds Central to be the primary resource you turn to in many later creative steps involving reviewing seeds. At those moments, you don't want to be hunting for lists. But the value it provides is more than just convenient access. The activity of consolidating seeds has the beneficial side effect of mixing up seeds of differing provenance and currency— juxtaposing seeds caught five years ago and five days ago. This is good! You want your system to reflect and honor the *timelessness* of seeds, relative to the flow of your life and especially to the *order in which you caught the seeds*.

Sorting and sifting is also productive work you *can* do when your creative fires are banked down rather than burning hot. And unlike real housework for most of us (vacuuming, anyone?), you can actually learn to enjoy *this* housekeeping time for its own sake. Yes, it's creative putter time, but you are also supporting and setting the stage for later flow-based creative work, with tasks you can do precisely when you lack the creative energy to do much else with the seeds themselves.

Of course, the work can also be energizing—which is an advantage but also a risk. Consolidating older lists will inevitably remind you of great ideas for songs you had and forgot (that's why you wrote them down!), and may therefore inspire you to start immediately working one of those seeds into a song. You can certainly go with this impulse, and hopefully wind up with a good song. But if you jump into writing a song every time you start consolidation work, you may never dig back all the way through those older lists to "touch" those seeds; and you won't get in the habit of going to Seeds Central for seeds to work on. This is why I advocate maintaining two distinct work practices: Sort and Sift, and Appointments with Inspiration.

Handling Seeds Many Times

Given all these different lists, you will likely wind up processing or handling a given seed multiple times. That might mean physically copying handwritten seeds again; working digitally, you might copy and paste. Either way, it's still *work*. But it's good work.

A maxim advanced in some general time and work organizing regimes is to "touch" materials only once if possible. The idea is to avoid making repeated decisions about practical items—pieces of mail, articles to sort, invitations to accept or decline and toss. But creative material—seeds, as well as later-stage material such as drafts and versions—is simply different. For one thing, song seeds are not pieces of mail we can decide goes in "do now," "do later," "archive," or "throw in trash" piles. Seed lists are *possibilities*—"might-do" rather than "to-do" lists.

In addition, because seeds involve *creative* content, "handling them"—and handling them multiple times—is part of the creative work itself. Song seeds are timeless because they are reviewed by creatures (us) who are changed by time. You are a different person, and writer, as you come back to a seed looked at before. Each time we review a seed, we respond in a different moment, and we see different possibilities. A seed that didn't strike you before might strike you differently this time, or you may now have the skills needed to develop that seed. You might jot down a title as a teenager that you can't tackle (or even understand!) until your sourpuss sixties.

Repeated auditioning and experience further change our perception of the material. Whether or not we go on to develop the seed at that time, simply transcribing it again will subtly shift and polish the seed content. And we too are changed by the encounter; each time you read back a lyric seed, or sing through a melody, you reinforce and shape new pathways in your songwriter's mind. This is an example of what neuroscience research calls *effortful encoding*. If, in some distant future, months from now, subcutaneous digital implants allow us to instantly store song seeds by mental projection into a single, elegantly organized virtual bin in a songwriters' temple in a video-game landscape, I think we will have a problem. This is supposed to be messy—and you're supposed to have to work at it a little harder than that.

For all these reasons, "handle once" just isn't all that helpful a principle to apply to song seeds.

A seed might first get scrawled in your pocket notebook, then transcribed by hand into the end pages of that season's songwriting journal, and from there transferred to a computer seed file. This is not wasted work, especially if you are doing some transformation of the seeds as you handle them. Of course, you don't want a workflow so inefficient that you are forced to copy and recopy seeds endlessly. Establish a clear sense of an *order* to your various sources of captured seeds, so that you always see a chain that leads you, ultimately, back to Seeds Central (unless the seed gets planted in a song along the way).

Consolidation Activities

As you review your seeds, you alternate between a set of related consolidation tasks.

Get Seeds onto a Single List

You might have notebook pages or files with just single seeds, others that list several or many seeds, some randomly jumbled, and some project- or context-specific lists. You may have used the word "SEED" in the title or first line, or used the location to indicate that. As you consolidate, you'll have a target list (which should be further "downstream"—as your seeds flow, in a beautiful river of mixed metaphors, toward the great ocean of Seeds Central).

Seed Sweeps

As you first try out some of the "good housekeeping" practices recommended in this book, you might be motivated to go "ninja seed catcher" for a while—to do a super-humanly thorough initial sweep through all those scraps of paper and stray seed lists, especially the ephemeral one-time lists you don't intend to use as part of your continuing practice. Begin with an inventory of all the weird places you have written down seeds, to date. Gather seeds from all those places. If they are physically removable, put them in a heap. Otherwise, commit to copying them into one central place.

An initial sweep of this sort might be one of the only ways you get all the way back to some older lists. Consolidation activities can be done in small increments, but it is natural to turn to more recent seed lists first. This is fine in and of itself; even if not worked in strict chronological order, working with these lists will feel fresher. But you want to regularly revisit older lists, as well. Good song seeds are essentially timeless—not dependent on your current emotional state or romantic adventures—so it is sometimes particularly potent to work with older seeds. Whether you consolidate via mighty housecleaning or small tidying efforts, make a practice of alternating between *newest* and *oldest* lists in your cleanup and consolidation activities.

If you are familiar with general workflow management systems (such as David Allen's Getting Things Done method), you may recognize Seed Sweep as a songwriter's version of Allen's recommended first steps for getting rid of your myriad separate to-do lists and action items. Though a dramatic initial effort can be intensely satisfying and energizing, don't let the thorough be the enemy of the helpful. Your sweep need not be complete and exhaustive. The goal is not to sweep you off your feet but to get you *on* your feet—to get you using the new system, the new container. And even with a mighty starting push, you will need to keep "collecting collections" into, or in the general direction of,

Seeds Central. So, find time for periodic, more modest sweeps. In particular, after you have had to improvise and collect material in a more haphazard way, use a sweep to get yourself back on track.

Allow for Unsorted Seeds

The lowest-energy consolidation work is simply gathering seeds from scattered places into one central area. My Seeds Central contains a "holding tank" bin for Unsorted Seeds. That means I'll need to do further sorting and sifting within Seeds Central itself.

By the way, although I mention sorting, one form of reorganization I don't do all that often is reordering or resequencing seeds in a given list—for example, alphabetically. This might help you find duplicates, but if your seed-catching practice is tight, you won't have many, except perhaps that odd ghost melody you keep hearing "for the first time" on multiple occasions.

Categorize Seeds

As you handle, in one review session, multiple seeds originally captured in separate, piecemeal fashion, common themes and groupings will emerge. In Seeds Central, you will want to establish some high-level categories—essentially "bins" that you toss the seeds into as you review them.

Some generic categories are good practice for any songwriter. You will want to distinguish seeds of different types: lyric, melodic, harmonic, etc. I further sift lyric seeds into song titles, good individual lines, individual words I find intriguing, idioms or clichés I could "flip" for a song, and concepts not yet phrased in compelling lyric form, such as story ideas, themes, bits of conversation, etc.

Make Up New Categories

In addition to these more universal categories, every songwriter should have some highly individual categories for seeds. I have a category called "Special Collections," with subcategories like "Songs of Conscience Ideas," "Chiasmuses (Chiasmi?)," and "I Was a Weird Little Kid" (yes, there is more than one seed in that list).

I also have higher-order seeds, as it were: ideas for an album, a song cycle, or other projects that would involve multiple songs. I sort these into different bins, because I will handle them differently (as discussed in chapter 10, "Working with Multiple Seeds").

Have fun with your categories! They can spark and encourage your creativity. For example, I keep separate lists for lines for songs, funny lines, and off-color lines. (No, I won't give you examples of the latter!) I don't try to make these distinctions when I *catch* seeds; that would be disastrous! But as I process them, I find that providing named lists for outside, risky, outrageous ideas encourages me to not reject them—and remembering that makes me braver about catching them in the future. In a sense, such categories represent layered notions of public versus private "imagined audiences" for the seeds. It's vital that somewhere at the core of your seed lists are areas where you can be absolutely fearless—knowing that, if you choose, those seeds need never see the light of day. (They are as safe as—I don't know, emails . . .)

Sometimes inventing (or perhaps recognizing) a new category for seeds will inspire you to sift through your Unsorted Seeds bin for more seeds for that new category. I've also found that creating a seed category makes me attentive in the future to seeds of that type. Once I had started a list of "Fiddle Tune Titles Inspired by My Cats," I began to find an endless parade of potential cat fiddle-tune names: "Making Little Things Scream" or "Meaty Fresh" (referring to the beef-flavored toothpaste we got from the vet). Often, making a new category and sifting seeds into it will spark a cascade of new seed ideas on the spot, which you can just add to the list.

Guidelines for Seed Wrangling

Allow for Imperfection

As I've said, I would minimize thinking about categorizing seeds when you catch them. You don't want to impede the process with any second-guessing. But even as I sort and sift, I don't agonize too much about whether I've correctly categorized a seed. As long as the seed is not lost or irretrievable, it's not an issue, and your idea of how to work with a seed may shift anyway once you start that work.

Adjust Your System

However you set up your song seed–catching protocol, it will inevitably be imperfect and messy. You will always be setting up new rules and conventions, then breaking or tweaking them. So, cleanup is perennially necessary, but this cleanup activity itself is important and useful, and can be fun!

The Tool Matters

Because sorting and sifting requires a lot of moving stuff around, it helps to do it in a tool that supports that kind of activity. Here, I find digital has an advantage over paper media. I keep my Seeds Central in an outliner program. I like this format rather than a plain text editor because I like list items I can easily drag around and reorder. Some outliners also provide a main text field and a subsidiary description field, a nice place to store ancillary information such as the context in which the seed was captured, quick notes about development angles, etc.

Caveat: Outliners support arbitrary levels of hierarchies—categories, subcategories, sub-subs, etc. I am a hierarchy/taxonomy nerd. I acknowledge that I am powerless over categories; I love sorting things into deep hierarchies—often too deep. Others prefer flat lists, especially with the powerful search capabilities now available. You'll want to find your own sweet spot in terms of where your categories spark your creativity, and where they start to be too fussy or make it harder to find things.

Delegating—Or Not

As you contemplate what may seem to be the largely clerical work of cleaning up and transferring seed lists, you may consider having someone else help out with some of these tasks. Certainly, depending on the scale of your songwriting work, you may want to work with a support person, especially for catalog management tasks such as those we will discuss in chapter 9.

At various times, I have had assistants type in song seeds off scraps of paper and journal lists. While this did save me time, I came to realize that the transcription work of handling seed material—even multiple times—is, in fact, an essential, if background, part of the creative work of songwriting. If you hand off or delegate certain stages of these activities, you may lose some of the value of having collected the material in the first place. At the very least, the categorizing and "sifting" work is essential. No act of transcription is truly neutral; there is always some interpretation, some transformation going on. Transcribing seeds awakens memory and triggers associative connections. Even if you don't immediately work a seed into a song draft (e.g., an Appointment with Inspiration as discussed below), you are—literally, I believe—shaping the neural pathways of your Songwriter Mind by handling the material, then handling it again. That work is yours to do.

APPOINTMENT WITH INSPIRATION

Seed catching is training in a specific mode of peripheral attention. With practice, you may reach a point where you begin to feel you can catch seeds almost at will—when you do set aside time to write or co-write, seed catching has "primed" your brain to the degree that you are likely to find inspiration on the spot, in the room. Your archived seed list is still there as a backup, but increasingly you will not depend on it, or *need* it to get started. Funny problem, huh?

The problem is not that *some* seeds you've captured won't get turned into songs. According to the Songwriter's Law of Abundance, you will—you must—collect many more seeds than you will ever turn into songs. Nor is seed-catching practice supposed to make you more dependent on seeds to get started.

The problem is rather if *no* seeds you capture are getting turned into songs. This outcome sucks, because, what about all those seeds? You must be fair to your seeds if you want them to stay potent!

And the problem is not just losing seeds in the mists of the lists. The larger problem is that the system itself will eventually erode. As you add seeds to your list, you tell yourself they will become great songs. But eventually, your Songwriter Mind (who knows you too well) knows you are lying—that a seed thrown on that list may disappear, never to be heard from again. In a panic, you start to squirrel away favored or high-anxiety seeds, so you won't forget them. Eventually, you'll stop contributing to and maintaining your lists, subverting, and finally abandoning, the system.

When you build your workflow around a container that you put stuff into, but you never take stuff out, you are essentially creating a *stale* or orphaned resource. To make an externalized resource into a trusted system, you must establish a regular practice of going back to that resource. Your workflow must guarantee every seed in Seeds Central a fighting chance of at least getting *considered* for a song. To ensure this, we need more than writing situations where we turn to seeds for a particular project need. We also need to make a practice of not just catching but also working with seeds, setting aside regular time for this work.

I call this an *Appointment with Inspiration* (AWI): a designated time to go back to your seed list with no agenda or project goal other than to find a seed that inspires you at that moment and "germinate"—write from—that seed. That tells your songwriter mind that this list is *active*. You could do your AWI with any seed lists, but the practice has the most value when applied to Seeds Central. Similarly, you can combine an AWI with a co-writing session, but I suggest doing it first as solo work.

Any AWI session, even if spontaneously initiated, should yield a promising start to a song, and will build your confidence in the usefulness of your song seed lists. But ideally, you will set up AWIs as regular appointments, not dependent on shifting outer opportunities or projects, or on your own fluctuating energy and enthusiasm. As we'll see, other practices will help you draw on your seed lists for specific projects. The deeper value of the AWI is for you to fully appreciate the power of starting a writing session with a seed you *already know* is a strong idea for you—that's why you caught it as a seed! By picking a specific seed to work on that matches your energy in the moment, you combine strong content with strong support from your context. In other words: don't schedule an AWI because you feel like writing a song. Come to trust that you will feel like writing a song *because* you scheduled an AWI. That said, you can maximize your chances for success by setting your AWI appointments for times and places that are responsive to your natural rhythms of creative work. (For my AWI practice, I prefer "after first awakening" time, the most sacred creative time for me.)

Each AWI session will have a common rhythm and flow. At the start of each session, simply scan down your chosen list, waiting for the first seed that sufficiently sparks your creative interest. That sparked collision of seed and interest might reflect your energy and focus, your emotional state, or myriad other factors. *You just need to find that seed, dodge the shirk, and get to work!*

Don't cheat and save out a favorite new seed you'll "work on for your next AWI session." This subverts the power of your seed list, and the serendipity and responsiveness of selecting the seed as the initial work of each session. When you have a creative task at hand, or a project agenda, you will also scan seeds. In that scenario, it makes sense to scan through the whole list and collect a queue of candidates. It matters that you find the best seed of what you have to choose from, to work toward that task goal. But an AWI has no goal other than drawing an energizing seed from the list to work on for a while. I do find, though, that the seed I choose to work on often reveals itself with an unmistakable, distinct response, not a vague "Should I pick this one or that one?" feeling. Be attentive for a seed that leaps out at you, resonates strongly, and connects by association with other material you have been working on.

You can experiment with setting a time limit for your AWI session, or letting the session expand based on the song draft you initiate. As with other writing practices (e.g., Pat Pattison's object writing technique), setting a time limit has two advantages: it builds skills for working rapidly and immersively, and it increases your willingness to schedule more sessions—you know the time limit puts a constraint on what you're committing to.

Similarly, you can play with different approaches to combining, or linking, AWIs and Sort and Sift sessions. It might be effective to set aside time for an AWI right after some consolidation work; you'll just have handled the seeds, and one is likely to spark inspiration in the moment. I'd suggest you commit to consolidating for a set time, tagging seeds that spark your interest as you go. When you've done your housekeeping, you might reward yourself with time to work on one of those seeds. But remember, these activities are meant for very different times in terms of your creative energy and focus. It's good to schedule some AWIs at different times than any housekeeping on seed lists, and vice versa.

ORGANIZING SEED LISTS FOR ACTION

As you sort and sift seeds and consolidate them in Seeds Central, some categories will be based on the seeds themselves, either by content (what the seeds are about) or type (lyric vs. melodic seeds, etc.). You can also pre-sort and pre-select seeds based on the kinds of creative work you expect to do with them. This will usually be done with a specific project context already in mind.

A song seed is a possibility. But sometimes, we generate or catch seeds with a specific project in mind—even if we're not yet writing the song. Pragmatically, we need to handle these seeds in a different way; there is a time- and opportunity-scoped action associated with them. It's one thing to resist putting a seed in the "bank" because you're afraid you might never find it again, in a grand philosophical workflow sense—it's another thing to know you'll need that seed next week. So it's a good idea to have a few containers for catch-all "Urgent Seeds," "Seeds for Current Projects," etc.

You will also want project-specific seed lists as queues for current work. These lists will need to be tied into whatever system you use to track current projects. But in any case, if you generate a seed with a specific active project in mind, do *not* add that seed into an overall seed workflow designed to handle inspiration-driven seeds, and expect to access it efficiently for your project. If you catch such a seed in your seed notebook, *annotate* it so that, as you sift and sort later, you know to divert that seed to the project list instead of to Seeds Central.

Later in this book, we will describe situations later in the life cycle of the song where the various seed lists introduced here get put to use: in developing and revising songs (chapters 5 and 6), in co-writing (chapter 7), and for reflective work and larger creative projects, where we can work with seeds not only individually, but also in the aggregate (chapter 10).

Figure 4.1 provides a summary of the basic workflow for handling seed and source material discussed so far.

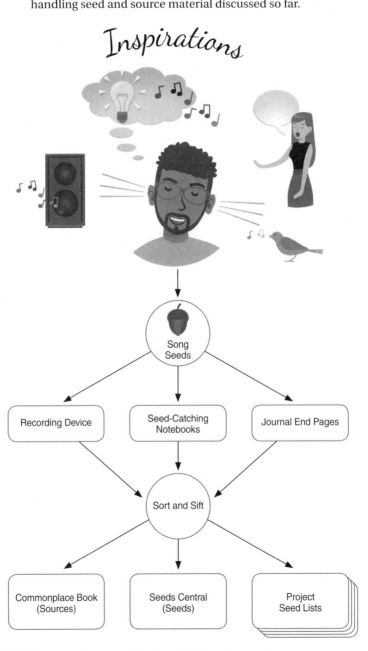

FIG. 4.1. Summary of Workflow for Seed and Source Material

CHAPTER 5

Developing Songs

We have discussed initial stages of collecting inspirations for songs: both original seeds and external sources. Now we are ready to *do the work*: start writing a song.

As we manage this workflow, we must contend with distinctive aspects of the songwriting process, such as the general challenges of messiness and abundance of material discussed in chapter 2. In addition, we face the challenges of reconciling fundamentally linear and chronological work products with a creative process with very different attributes:

- **Non-linear.** We may create material for a song in a sequence quite different from that experienced by the listener in the final song. Writing from a title seed, for example, we may work from title to chorus; from there, we may write a first verse, which turns out to be the last verse. Beginnings are sometimes the last to get written!

- **Divergent.** Especially in earlier, more generative stages of writing, we may produce far more material than is destined for the final song, as well as "pre-writing" material (prose free writing, rhyme worksheets, etc.).

- **Iterative.** Most songs develop via a series of sketches, drafts, versions, and revisions. Work on these versions—adding, removing, rearranging, and transforming material—often unfolds over a period of time, in different working sessions. You might develop a lyric seed into a first verse, come back later and add music, later bring that fragment to a co-writer, etc.

- **Indeterminate.** The writing and revision process is not an engineering process. It sometimes requires multiple passes and even retreats back to earlier versions. At the same time, we can get lost in that work, and wind up feeling like we are chasing our own tails. We need markers to let us know we are moving forward—or that we're stuck.

- **Multi-stranded.** Songwriters often work on multiple songs during the same period—with a single working session sometimes yielding material for different songs. These song "strands" may be at different stages of completion (including "stranded"!).

Besides these qualities, the rhythms of songwriting often shift between very different kinds of creative work:

- **Generation and assemblage.** As we are working on a song, we may be generating brand new material, sifting back through previous versions and fragments, or even turning to song seed lists to look for matching material.

- **Attention.** Working on a song involves weaving between a direct task focus and more peripheral, free-flowing work. The latter type of work often generates material that is not usable in the song at hand—even new seeds.

- **Evaluation.** As we generate material, we are also reviewing, evaluating, and self-critiquing or, in co-writing or review settings, receiving critique from others.

- **Creation and reflection.** As we write songs, we are also learning our craft, and often want to capture reflective material to support that learning as well.

KEY WORKFLOW DESIGN DECISIONS

Given these characteristics, we need to make some key design decisions about the types of work products and practices we employ to catch this songwriting tiger by the tail. These decisions involve the specific media and formats by which we capture creative material:

- Paper vs. digital
- Writing text free-hand vs. typing (or thumbing!)
- Capturing material in text vs. audio or video form
- Loose-leaf vs. bound format
- Using pen vs. pencil and eraser
- Destructive editing vs. journaled or snapshot versions
- Side-by-side vs. interleaved layouts

Consider these as *architectural* decisions: each choice shapes many different products (containers) and activities. Though framed separately here, these choices also intertwine in sometimes subtle ways. I can clarify the choices but I can't recommend a single "best practice." What works for you will depend on your own preferred working style and habits, and your choices will evolve over time. But make no mistake: no matter how you are writing songs right now, you *have* made these decisions—whether explicitly or implicitly, by default or through inattention. It's worth rethinking and making these choices more intentionally, for these seeming details can have a profound impact on the overall quality and productivity of your songwriting.

YOUR SONGWRITING JOURNAL

In a cubbyhole in my messy office at home, three shelves overflow with just shy of 200 journals I've kept over the course of my life: personal diaries, song journals, tune manuscript books, sketchbooks with fledgling attempts at artwork (never my strong suit), dream journals, journals of *I Ching* readings, travel journals, project notebooks for ambitious projects commenced and never finished, teaching notebooks, and even notebooks full of Nashville Number System chord progressions for my "Hank Williams in Hell" song challenges. (Contact me for details!)

No artifact is more personal to you as a songwriter than your songwriting journal. Of course, if you write many songs and write for many years, you will eventually fill many journal volumes. So, by your *journal*, I mean the style of artifact, material, and format you adopt as a continuing journal practice. This practice is likely to change over time.

One major choice many songwriters make at some point is to *separate* their song journals from their personal diaries. It can be illuminating to reflect back on the time when you made that shift (if you have)—or if you have not, to envision how making such a shift might recolor your approach to your songwriting. But in any case, your song journals—however interwoven with other journals and diaries—and the ways your journal practice has shifted over time can provide you (and don't forget your Future Biographers!) a true Memory Theater: an amazing retrospective on your creative work, as well as your life and biography.

Song Journal Format

I'll describe the song journal format that generally works well for me. I never seem to get it *exactly* right, or stick with whatever my current system is *exactly* as I'm supposed to! So, I continue to tinker with and fine-tune the format with each new journal. To support that continued polishing and evolution, I reserve a blank page at the front of the journal, after the table of contents, to review the journal after it's finished. I debrief what worked well, what was problematic, and new conventions or annotations I started using.

I keep numbered, chronologically ordered physical bound journals for my songs and instrumental compositions. (Because music drafts often involve staff notation, I find it convenient to keep separate notebooks for these.) I intermix solo and co-written song sessions in my song journal.

Chronologically ordered journals provide substantive documentation of creative work for legal purposes; it would be ludicrous to try to falsely recreate a song draft in such an archival format. It hasn't come up, but it's comforting to know the documentation is there. Chronological ordering of the journals also helps me track progress and productivity, locate drafts from past co-writing sessions, etc. I also love the satisfying ritual of seeing a bound journal fill up with songs, and eventually seeing a shelf fill up with journals. (I have not yet filled a wall with shelves of journals, but I'm working on it.)

Call me old-school, but I believe there is tremendous power in *writing things down by hand.* That physical engagement of hand, eye, shape, color, etc., is important for any kind of writing, including song lyrics. I acknowledge (and certainly hope!) that this book will be read by songwriters from generations that grew up from infancy with digital technology, for whom it may feel most natural to do even initial writing and sketching digitally. Even so, I urge you to explore writing *by hand*, and to designate a physical *container* for your songwriting work. Try it, and observe the effects on your work.

For you as a songwriter, your journal archive is one of your most valued physical artifacts, even if you eventually scan or transcribe all the material from those journals into digital form.

So indulge yourself and invest in good-quality materials for your journals. Consider this: if you fill 200 notebooks in your lifetime, you'll have spent a few thousand dollars to secure your intellectual property legacy. (And imagine how happy those Future Biographers will be!)

I use journals with unlined, archival-quality acid-free paper, heavy enough not to have ink bleed through the pages. Often, this involves buying the sorts of sketchbooks used by visual artists for watercolors, ink drawings, etc.

Journal Layout

When I begin a journal, I set it up in the following way:

- I maintain a spreadsheet index of my journals to date. When I "initiate" a new journal, I give it an entry in that spreadsheet. That assigns the new journal to the next number in my rolling index. I write this number on the title page of the journal, and on a label or two which I stick on the outside of the journal, so I can see it at a glance.

- I like to give each of my journals a "fanciful title." This is my personal bit of humor: my chance to be pretentious, artsy-fartsy, surrealistic, or nonsensical. It also gives each journal a bit of its own personality. As a way to avoid taking yourself too seriously, I highly recommend giving each of your journals its own unique Purposefully Pompous Title Page.

- On the title page, I note the date I "commence" each new journal. At the end, as I fill in the last page, I note the date of the last entry as well (usually with a celebratory bit of whimsy). Thus, the journal's title page shows a date range telling me the rough chronology of the journal in my series. Sometimes, I have multiple journals (for different types of material) overlapping in range.

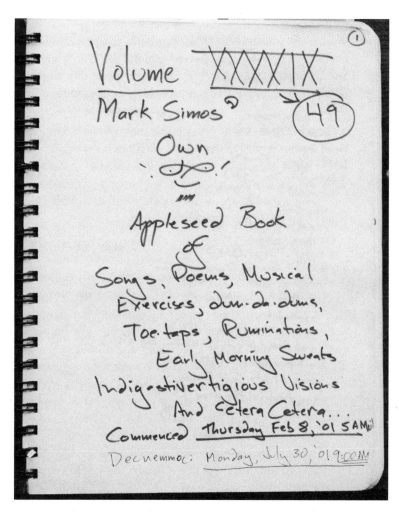

FIG. 5.1. Songwriting Journal Title Page

Journal Table of Contents

As I became accustomed to my journal architecture, I learned to leave a few blank pages at the front of each journal for a table of contents, which I update periodically as I fill the journal (or sometimes afterward). In an ideal process, I would update the TOC conscientiously after every entry. In real life, the updating often lags well behind the rate at which I'm filling the journal. But I've found this bit of raggedness in the process to be helpful:

in low-energy moments, the simple act of going through my journal and updating the table of contents can be a calming and encouraging way to review recent material and keep it active. It's another way of "touching" my work. Remember, with *creative* as opposed to *business* materials, touching things multiple times is *good*.

Eventually, there's an entry in the table of contents for each work session. A session entry is a contiguous set of pages created in a single session, for a single song. If I started a second song in the same session, that becomes a new entry. If I work on a song over several sessions, those are separate entries as well. Here is what I record for each session entry:

- **Item Number.** I like to know how many sessions of work are represented in the journal. This is a nice easy metric. It also gives me a reference point for that entry, for example, for a session that was a *revision* of a song from an earlier entry.

- **Type of Work.** Since I often have different kinds of material in one journal, I like to indicate whether a given entry is a new "Song" versus a "Revision" of a song started earlier.

  I might also follow creative work with a "Reflection" about the song or the process. Depending on the scope and focus of the journal, I indicate other types of entries I want to keep track of, like "Teaching Note," "Theory," "Poem," "Project" (an idea for a new project), etc. Including entry types as labels in the contents allows for the fact that my separation of content into different journals will always be a little messy.

- **Title.** A working title to remind me of the song content—sometimes just a placeholder.

- **Date.** I tend to date even entries that don't have much date sensitivity in terms of copyright status. The table of contents shows me how time flowed in that journal.

- **Page Range.** In some ways, this is the most important information in the table of contents! Until you've faced the challenge of finding some song you wrote sometime, looking at a bunch of journals, you won't appreciate how useful the locator is!

When you've worked on one song over several non-consecutive sessions in the journal, you have a choice: list each session separately, with "Revision" labels showing the thread of one song in development; or indicate separate page ranges in one entry. I prefer to let the table of contents roll more chronologically. Each way of working makes some things easier, and some harder, and thus will require some workarounds. For me, ultimately, the journal's value lies in its chronological "log" flow.

WORKFLOW: WRITING THE SONG

Having discussed the mechanics of how you use the journal, let's now consider the flow of the developing song. Though I've resolved not to stray into extensive discussions of craft, it's worth distinguishing some different kinds of working material, each with its own shapes and rhythms.

I generally do *first drafts* of songs, and often at least the first few revisions, in my journal.

Every time I write in my current journal, I treat it as a *work session*. I start on a fresh page (even if the last page wasn't completely filled) and number the page. I date each individual session entry (which will often run onto multiple pages). If I am elsewhere than my home writing environment, I also record *where* I'm writing. And if it's a co-write session, I record *all* co-writers involved in the session. (Since you'll often begin co-writing without knowing what song you'll write—if any!— the session information gets written first.) I then begin work on drafting the song.

I tend to interleave pre-writing content with song draft material. Pre-writing can include notes about the theme or subject matter, object writing, or any other prose or descriptive writing that is used in preparation for direct attempts at lyrics. If I'm co-writing, I'll also capture notes from the conversation. If I want to attend more closely to process issues, I use a left-page/ right-page format: song content goes on one side, reflections and decision notes on the other (as described in chapter 10). As I go to new pages in the same writing session, I put a *forward arrow* ($\rightarrow$) at the bottom of the current page, number the new page, and put a *forward arrow* at the top of that page. That gives me a clear visual clue that the song draft is continuing across multiple pages.

I write in pen, not pencil and eraser. This does not imply overconfidence or unwillingness to revise. Working in pen, I commit to and must be comfortable with revising by *writing again*, further down the page or on new pages (rather than erasing), leaving a trace of drafts and corrections behind. As I revise, I might cross out rejected or superseded lines, or mark cross-outs in the margin to avoid obscuring the text. Or, with several alternatives, I might mark the *preferred* version. In any case, intermediary attempts remain visible. This is only a problem if the preferred or final choice is not indicated. In a bound-journal format, chronological progress through the journal helps keep that clear.

I write in *black* pen, by the way, because it *copies* better than blue pen. Assume handwritten pages (whether in a bound journal or loose leaf) will eventually get scanned or copied. You might copy pages to share with co-writers, to collate related pages into a song-specific folder, or for a safety backup. (For the same reason, if you use manuscript paper, do *not* use paper with staff lines in light blue ink. They do not copy, and you will be left with notes of indeterminate pitch—great if you are following in the aleatoric footsteps of John Cage, not so great for fiddle tunes!) Note, however, that new technologies are making it possible to get the best of both worlds: the combined benefits of writing by hand on physical paper, and instant digital archiving of the material.

Once I've generated enough alternative lines, or juggled things around enough, such that I now need a visually clearer representation of what I have, I move forward to a clean page and assemble a temporary "working draft." This involves copying— by hand—preferred alternatives for each line. This handwork is *not* wasted effort; as I rewrite the line, I have a further chance to quietly sound it out and check that it's what I want. *Writing again* becomes an opportunity to *rewrite*. Often, a lot of subtle micro-editing, like dropping small filler words, happens in this stage, due to the seeming disadvantage of working by hand. This is a major difference between working by hand and in a digital medium. (In theory, you could manually retype text this way in a digital medium, but I'll wager you a thumb drive most of the time you won't; since you can copy and paste, you almost always *will* copy and paste.)

When I run out of steam, or think I'm done, or otherwise feel I've reached the end of the song work for that session, instead of a forward arrow, I put a star at the end of the entry on the last page. If I know it's work in progress, I might write something like "TBC" (to be continued) to indicate that the song's not done.

Starting Seeds

When working from seed to song, a good baseline assumption is that each seed provides the genesis for a *separate* song. It's important to keep this in mind when working with seed lists, which are in general unstructured and unordered. A list per se is not intended to suggest contiguous lines of songs in sequence, or even lines destined for the same song. Sifting, sorting, categorizing, and rearranging seeds helps reinforce this. It's like a big card shuffle, where gradually seeds that were gathered around the same time or in the same context drift away from each other—unless you have reasons to keep them gathered. And conversely, seeds with little or no connection bump up against each other in proximity. It's about as non-linear as you can get!

Each different kind of seed material will lend itself to different development techniques. A good rule of thumb, though, is to actually transfer the seed material from where it lives in the seed list into the working material (journal, studio session, etc.) where you will be developing it. If you already captured some sketches of development ideas with the seed, bring them over as well. But sometimes you might need to jettison some of this material and approach the seed with fresh ears. If your starting point is a messier fragment, such as the "morsels" we discuss in chapter 6, you might need to do even more excavation work of this kind.

Pre-Writing

Since many songs start from concepts and ideas, good songwriting often involves generating supporting material *not* intended for direct incorporation in the song. Much songwriting pedagogy consists of various pre-writing tools and techniques of this sort.

A simple example is a *worksheet* (a technique many song-writers have become familiar with through Pat Pattison's *Writing Better Lyrics, 2nd Ed.* Writer's Digest Books, 2010). A rhyming dictionary (physical or digital) is an external tool or resource. Though you may create your worksheet in part through use of such a resource, it is your own product—an aid to lateral thinking, facilitating rapid brainstorming of multiple possibilities, instead of grabbing the first thing that comes to mind. Usually applied to lists of rhyme words, worksheets can also be created for synonyms, or words that fit a certain scene or landscape. You can see a master like Sondheim integrating this technique seamlessly into his sketches and drafts, in his books *Finishing the Hat* (Knopf, 2010) and *Look, I Made a Hat* (Knopf, 2011). Worksheets are generally prepared in the context of working on one song—but not always. Some writers gather lists, even physical boxes, of what are essentially worksheets—"sonic connection" studies—before they know for what song they will use them.

Whether you use loose-leaf pages, sequential pages in your notebook, or computer files, you'll need to manage pre-writing materials as part of your workflow design, with varied decisions. Do I save these materials after I've used them, or throw them out? Do I keep them with the individual song, or as a separate resource like a seed list? Do I share them with my co-writers? I often use a rhyme worksheet throughout the writing of the song, as in a verse-refrain song where new, ideally intensifying, rhymes are needed for the repeating refrain in multiple verses. I therefore tend to document them with other song materials.

Using Seed Lists in Writing

Earlier, I emphasized that a good starting assumption in working with seeds is "one seed, one song." You don't want to assume that a lyric idea, a melodic fragment, and a chord progression all grabbed around the same time—as seeds, that is—necessarily belong together in one song. That said, in many situations in both solo and co-writing, seed lists remain useful in the work of developing the song.

At any stage in working on a song when new material is required for a next creative step, you have a few recurring alternatives:

- Generate new material "on the fly."
- Steal material from elsewhere in the song. (Stealing is always good, but the shorter the trip across the rooftops the better.)
- Review material from previous drafts.
- Associatively recall previous seed material that might fit.
- Look back through various seed lists for appropriate material.

Each of these strategies requires good songwriting craft and technique. But the last few strategies—looking back through previous drafts, and especially using seed lists—can be potent accelerators of creative work. To be effective, however, these techniques not only require craft and a good sense for the integrity of the resulting work, but also depend heavily on the supporting seed practices discussed in chapter 4 and on the revision practices we will discuss in chapter 6.

Finding Seeds by Association

Let's say you've started from a title seed and have developed that seed into a chorus lyric. You might then write new music for that chorus in response to the lyric. But this is often also a moment where you spontaneously remember, by association, a sectional chord progression previously captured as a seed sketch. At that juncture, you want to be able to find your way quickly to that progression. Here is where having done the prior work of consolidation, annotation, and categorization serves you well. You might find that progression in your Seeds Central, sorted into a "Harmonic Seeds" category, perhaps annotated with a comment like "good for an uptempo chorus." If you've recently done a seed sweep, you might have reminded yourself of that progression even though it was written a while ago. The workflow management activities directly contribute to your effective use of that fragment.

NOTE: In my experience, it is more typical to find your way back to musical seeds by association, which is why preserving the time and date context for audio sketches is useful in ways not as essential to working with lyric seeds.

Finding Seeds by Scan-and-Match

You can also go back to your seed lists without a specific seed in mind. You can scan rapidly through a number of seeds, keeping in the foreground the criteria for the kind of material you are trying to fit with or match. I call this "Cinderella's slipper" approach *scan-and-match*.

Obviously, there is no guarantee there will be a match, or a "perfect match" (whatever that means). But your workflow management practices do provide advantages:

- You're searching through material that you have already prescreened as holding intrinsic interest for you.
- If you've been an assiduous seed catcher, you are playing the odds not with a mere handful of candidate seeds, but with dozens or even hundreds. (That means, by the way, that you will want to be able to scan through them quickly.)

Scan-and-match techniques are particularly useful at certain points in writing:

- When moving to material in a new facet, e.g., starting to add a chord progression to a lyric, or looking for a lyric title to match a musical section.
- When moving to a new musical section, e.g., looking for a verse or pre-chorus melody to complement a chorus melody already written.
- When a desired transition can tolerate, or actually requires, a high degree of contrast, or a shift in the modality or tone of the material.

You might be looking for material that matches in a direct way, e.g., reflecting the same emotional content as the current material in the song. But sometimes, you are looking for more surprising and edgy juxtapositions of material, such as music that runs counter to the lyric tone in an ironic but effective way. The very "crap shoot" nature of scan-and-match can sometimes provide this sort of creative "collision" stimulus.

You do have to train yourself to not accept a match too readily. Laziness, or a natural desire to celebrate the serendipity, can mute your critical appraisal. Is this *really* the right melody or chords? To avoid this, review *all* constraints on the match you're looking for. For example, a musical seed won't only need to match the lyrics you have on hand, but it also needs to dovetail with the theme and story, characters and regional flavor, genre, or style. Scan-and-match actually works best the *more* restrictions you put on the match. You're looking not for a kinda-sorta match, but for that satisfying "snick" of a jigsaw piece fitting into the gap. Be choosy.

Also, don't stop with the first acceptable match you find. Unlike an AWI, where your goal is just to find a seed that sparks your interest, here you have a context with tight selection criteria. So, scan until you have a few candidates. Then try them in context, serially, before deciding which fits best. Even clear mismatches may provide valuable clues about what's needed.

One last word of caution, to avoid the impression that I am advocating a "paint by numbers" approach to your songwriting. I love the non-linearity of weaving previously caught seeds into new writing. But pick moments to try scan-and-match with care. It's fine to scan-and-match when you are drawing a blank and don't have any fresh ideas readily at hand, or if you've made a few sketches but they're just not clicking for you, or when you have run out of momentum for more direct generative work. (In theory, you could scan-and-match even before trying to generate material on the fly, or if you have something you think is pretty good but want to see, "Can I beat this or complete this?") But don't turn to your seed lists as soon as you hit any sort of block. If new material needs to resonate closely with what you've already got—and it's simply hard to find—don't short-circuit the process. You might need to stick with it: find out why you're stuck, dig deeper, and do the new writing.

Sketches

Great artists—in any form, any medium—do not settle for their first draft. At every stage of creative work, they generate and evaluate. As they work, they attend to reactions and responses, but do not let them interrupt the flow of their work. Rather, they carry that new insight into a next iteration.

I call this activity of generating multiple, consecutive, and immediate attempts for any given creative step *sketching*. I use the word by analogy to visual artists' notebooks. An artist's sketch is by nature not a finished product, not a testament to static perfection, but a rapid impressionistic attempt—a light outlining, leaving out details to be filled in later. Some artists sketch in pencil, then erase, redraw, and smudge. But many sketches retain multiple, superimposed contours, making (or leaving) visible the artist's approximating progression toward a desired image or effect. The artist traces the contour of an arm or a tree—makes an attempt—and then, *without erasing*, tries again . . . and again. Sketching is about again-ness.

Sketching is an essential component of great songwriters' work practice. A key principle of virtuoso sketching in songwriting— not unlike multiple takes in studio recording—is to learn not to stop with the first attempt that feels "good enough." If you're after "great," good enough isn't good enough!

I vividly recall a Berklee clinic with hit songwriter Dean Pitchford, mentioned earlier. Describing working on the lyrics for songs written for the movie *Footloose*, he held up two fingers, about one and a half inches apart, to show the students the height of the stack of yellow-pad pages for rewrites of just *one* song, done over a six- or seven-week period. Eyebrows raised and jaws dropped. The gap between those fingers eloquently conveyed to the aspiring writers in that room what it meant to do serious, intensive drafting and revision on a song.

Sketching takes on particular importance in songwriting, since song structure often includes varied repetitions. As you sketch, you are looking not just for a best choice for one occurrence. As with a worksheet, you might wind up using several of the alternatives within the song. In addition, choices made in songwriting are not fixed in stone. It is good to revise, but also good to remember that revision is not infallible. An earlier version second-guessed or overthought, or a discarded alternative, might be revealed later as a stronger choice than your replacement. Sketching preserves these earlier alternatives.

Sketching requires leaving traces behind. This can be harder for some writers than others, due to natural differences in proclivities and working style. Some like to do as much revision and editing as possible "in their head," only externalizing material once it feels fairly formed. Others are willing to capture material in a more flow-based way, trusting they can edit and remove later. Such differences can lead to complex dynamics in co-writing. (In my collaboration classes, we call this the polarity of "stewers" vs. "spewers.")

While there is no right or wrong in such temperamental contrasts, I believe that, because of the importance of sketching in songwriting, there is an edge or advantage to an approach that favors externalizing, capturing, and *not erasing*. This has direct impact on workflow practice. It echoes the physical writing choice of working in pen versus pencil, but digital technology has made the issue more acute, due to the ubiquity of *destructive editing*. You type in text, think better of it, delete it, and type in a new version. What you have just done is the digital analogue of *writing in pencil, using an eraser, and writing over what you have done*. Only the digital eraser is perfect; the previous version is gone. Working digitally doesn't prevent sketching, but it makes it very easy—too easy—not to do.

Whether working in pen in a physical journal, or editing a digital file, songwriters benefit overall from a workflow style that allows sketches to remain "on the record." In the words of artist, activist, and teacher of creativity Corita Kent: "Save everything; it might come in handy later."

Audio Sketches

The sketches referred to so far apply largely to textual materials like lyrics. An equivalent kind of sketching happens when recording audio for a song, with lots of stops and starts, cycling back and trying different variations, etc. This is how compositional or "making stuff up" time flows as compared to performance time—like a stream running over a rocky bed, with lots of eddies and swirls. If you just leave your recorder running while working on a song or co-writing, you'll likely get an audio record of this sort. One caution here, though: remember that saving lots of stuff can be problematic if it is too hard to sift through later. Recently, I asked a student co-writing team how they had saved material from their writing session (which I had required to be two hours). They said they "just recorded the whole thing." I confess, I chuckled. Because unless they have photographic (phonographic?) memories, that great melody one of them sang—once—for the verse at precisely 1:23 into the session is now buried in an untagged two-hour recording, and might as well be lost. So, when recording while in sketching mode, it's good when you've done something memorable to immediately leave a tag or marker, or break the recording into named fragments you can later listen back to, knowing the chronology. In fact, audio recording this way can empower you to sketch more boldly. As you try alternatives, you can experiment and go further, without worrying that new ideas will overwrite promising earlier sketches in your short-term memory. If they do, you can go back to the audio record. When live-composing a two-part fiddle tune, a first part I like will feel unforgettable. Then, if I go on to make up a strongly contrastive second part, I often struggle to accurately retrieve that first part, even minutes later. So in sketching, in both solo and co-writing, be willing to go back to earlier fragments in the recording, even during the session itself. (This is an extraordinary advantage for modern songwriters and composers, compared to those from eras where memory and notation were the only ways to save ideas—but we must use that technology very strategically.)

SONG DRAFTS

Sketches by nature are messy: a series of fragments and alternatives, lines or phrases in different orders. You reach a fairly significant crossover point when you start to assemble a truer *draft* of your song. At this point, you are beginning to have a concept for the overall form of the song, though that concept can change and sectional material can still move around or get juggled internally in all sorts of ways. A *draft* is a version that presents a more consecutive presentation of the song. The changes in workflow between sketches and drafts necessitate different conventions and techniques for keeping track of things.

Cross-Outs vs. Bring-Alongs

When you are sketching, everything is only a possibility. In a draft, you place material as a working candidate. *Crossing material out* removes it; *bringing material along* (that is, forward into the working draft) is a way of including it. Crossing out assumes the rest of the material there is being kept; it is a notation that implies you're already working on a draft. So, you shouldn't need to cross out material from your sketches. Just leave it there, as your trace. Instead, carry that material forward (manually copy, or digitally copy and paste) into the draft. When working on a draft, the task is different. You are continually and actively reviewing the draft. In a handwritten draft, there are two nice things about crossing out: you can *still read what you wrote*, and you can also clearly see it was rejected.

Annotations

There are also occasions where you aren't rejecting the line outright, but need to record your evaluation and thoughts about the line. Here, *annotations* are useful. An annotation is any sort of "meta-information" about the material. In lyrics, it might be textual notes set apart by braces {} or brackets [], or separated by a dash after the line. In audio materials, it might be a marker in a track with a comment. Annotations could also indicate notations for rhyme or metric schemes you are using, to help you align the structure of parallel sections.

Alternatives

You can also annotate certain lines as *alternatives*. Annotations are useful at any stage of writing and on into demo production. For example, in the studio, a "comping sheet" is essentially a lyric sheet annotated with line-by-line indications of preferred takes for later "comping" and editing. In earlier stages of songwriting, you are comping not takes but alternatives for components of the song itself.

These alternatives can be of varying granularity, from individual words to entire sections. I might write alternative words or phrases in the margin, or include a phrase in brackets. It's helpful to distinguish *optional* material to be added from *alternative* material to replace what's in the main text. I use brackets to set off optional material, such as a word I suspect may not be needed but I still want to consider. I'll add a *backslash* "\" at the start of the bracketed phrase if it's a candidate to *replace* preceding material in the main text. Usually, the content makes clear how much would be replaced. Similar conventions can be useful later in "fair copy" versions, which represent a more permanent snapshot of the song at a particular milestone of progress. In a final lyric sheet, annotations might represent not pending decisions, but alternate versions that are part of the finished song.

Here's a brief example, from a co-write of mine with Sally Barris on the song "Crazy Good." [2] We had come up with these lines for the chorus:

There's crazy like a taxi driver
Crazy like your old friend Joe
Crazy like a [daddy] penguin
Keeping an [\his] egg warm in the snow

The bracketed text indicates decisions we were deferring, as of this particular draft. Often a decision is deferred when there are subtle tradeoffs and interactions of effects to consider. The first bracketed word—[daddy]—is *optional* text, to be included or not. It feels narratively important: it's cool that it's the *daddy* penguin keeping that egg warm. Yet the word rhythmically crowds the line. The second annotation—[\his]—is an *alternate*. Do we want "an egg" or "his egg"? The two decisions might interact: if we leave out "daddy" do we want the clue provided by the gendered "his"? Use annotations for options and alternatives when the matter's not sure yet—but it sure matters! (We'll return to this example when we discuss the Stewpot in chapter 6.)

Appraisal Annotations

Annotations can also document running appraisals and evaluations of the strengths of various lines. You might mark a difficult line with a "?" or "Can we beat this?" You can annotate not just lyrics this way, but also chord charts, lead sheets, or audio materials via comments placed in the timeline. (Some of my Nashville chord charts, with various "?" or "!" annotations after specific chords, start to look like the experts' annotations of moves in famous chess games!)

Such annotations can be invaluable in solo writing but also especially in co-writing. Songwriting is an inherently non-linear and iterative process, and artists with varying temperaments

---

2. Lyric excerpts from "Crazy Good" ©2008 Sally Barris/Wrensong (ASCAP) and Mark Simos/ Devachan Music (BMI).

and working styles handle divergent possibilities and contingent decisions in very different ways. Some writers lean toward internally mulling possibilities to a point of satisfaction before externalizing them. For them, the simple act of writing down a line can seem like a committed decision rather than capturing a possibility. Explicit annotation conventions that document the provisionality of certain lines can help such writers work more fluidly and responsively, without feeling that they are compromising.

Such annotations also become useful in later phases, as helpful reminders of still-open loops and decisions when returning to the song in a later (sometimes *much* later!) session. They are also valuable in self-critique, or for receiving and documenting peer critique. I don't usually mark "keepers" in my own writing—I hope *every* line is a keeper! But when facilitating peer critique, I usually begin by asking listeners to point out "golden moments": spotlighted lyrical or musical points, tied as closely as possible to a localized spot. It's as important to note these golden moments as the problem spots, to guide later revision.

Another useful annotation is noting "model" songs that often come to mind, especially during co-writing. These can be acknowledged reference songs you want to listen to for a feel or groove, or they may emerge as a discovered and unintended similarity to an existing song, warranting some caution to guard against unconscious borrowing. ("Wait! Are we totally ripping off this progression from that old Carpenters song?")

Placeholders: Dummies, Paraphrases, and Stubs

You can also use annotations as placeholders for material that is not there yet. These placeholders are important to place in the draft because the *place* is important in the draft! Placeholders help you keep the form clearly in mind, while also supporting non-linear and contingent working styles. Many a co-write session has ground to a halt unnecessarily, simply because writers got stuck trying to find a particular line instead of putting in a placeholder, moving on, and eventually coming back to it. (This seems obvious until you are the king losing a kingdom for want of a horseshoe nail—that one perfect line!)

It's helpful to distinguish a few different types of placeholders, and to evolve clear annotations for these in your own work practice:

- *Dummies* approximate desired sound, rhythm, or structural aspects, while not specifying content. If you know you need a four-stress line ending in a rhyme for "bars," you can write something like: "duh *dum* duh *dum* duh *dum* duh *–ars*." Dummies can range from templates of this sort, to nonsense lines, to half-sincere real attempts at the line. (If it's not an obvious dummy line, annotate that clearly; you never know what you might settle for later!)

- *Paraphrases* are reminders of *what* you want to say/sing but not *how* (that is, the sound and form) of how you'll say it. You paraphrase, in prose, a description of what the missing piece needs to do, semantically and narratively.

- A *stub* is a placeholder that stands in for a whole section, particularly useful when hashing out the overall form and flow of the song.

Here's an example of how these annotations might be used in a draft:

PRECHORUS 1:
I always thought my heart was made of stone
[I always expected that eventually I'd wind up ...] alone
u / u / u / u / u / u / u –ONE   +7
Expected that eventually I'd wind up all alone
. . .

[PRE-CHORUS 2: something hopeful about how it might turn out this time?]

I start with a draft line that establishes an end rhyme. For the second line, I have a following rhyme word, and know what I want the line to say, but don't have the lyric set rhythmically yet: a good place for a paraphrase. The third line shows a dummy, a rhythmic template, for the same target line. It's especially important to annotate here, because my intended rhythm *doesn't* match the preceding line. Instead, I want the line length to extend from five to seven stresses. The fourth line shown could be the final *second* line, satisfying both paraphrase and dummy, both removing and adding lyric material to bring sense and sound together. I also know I'll want a second, "through-written" prechorus (that is, with changing lyrics). I show that with a stub, and an annotation.

Some useful working materials that are *not* direct draft materials are essentially composites of these various types of placeholders. (We could consider these to be other kinds of pre-writing materials, except that they are often generated not "pre-," but during the drafting stage.)

- A *song form chart* is a summary representation of the song's form, essentially consisting of a sequence of sectional stubs, e.g., "INTRO V1 PRE CH BREAK . . . " It's often helpful to annotate this on the page alongside the lyrics, to keep the sectional context clear. When considering how to *shift* song form in revision, you might sketch (again!) several such charts consecutively.

- A *song plan* is a condensed draft that, in effect, annotates the stubs of a song form chart with paraphrases of anticipated narrative content for each section. One important addition of final lyric content is a phrase representing a hook (e.g., a refrain or chorus title), dropped in at appropriate places in the sectional stubs. This facilitates rapid appraisal of how well a repeating refrain or title will work in the flow of the song.

- There's a Nashville songwriter's trick called "Writing the Letter," where you prepare for a song (particularly a first-person, direct-address, situational song) by writing a prose "letter" from the singer to the one sung to. This technique is essentially a paraphrase, not of just one section, but perhaps of the whole song. It can even show up within the final song itself, such as the spoken *recitation* passages (prose or spoken lyric) heard in some old-school country songs (such as "Still" by Bill Anderson).

Notation in Song Drafts

Formal notation renderings for songs, including lead sheets (melody, lyrics, and chords notated on staff lines) and chord charts, are sometimes considered primarily as ways to formally document finished songs, or to communicate with session players and vocalists. Notation formats in use vary across genres and musical communities. In contemporary songwriting, especially in production-heavy styles, technology and recording environments have become primary de facto "notations."

Yet, more conventional forms of notation can play a significant role in developing the song. Such uses of notation may be unfamiliar, and at times daunting, for songwriters accustomed to creating in mostly intuitive, semi-improvised ways, via live performance and recording. But used at appropriate points in the process, notation can provide a powerful aid to the creative work of songwriting.

It's beyond our scope here to discuss detailed conventions for notations such as lead sheets and chord charts. Here, we'll focus primarily on implications for workflow management.

Notation Formats

How and when in the process you integrate notation into the workflow of developing songs will depend on your own skill levels and working style, and to some extent may also vary with the type of song and the expected performance and recording contexts. Specialized skills are required for each notation format, and these can present hurdles for many songwriters. Notation programs like Finale and Sibelius provide support for many of these formats, and can perform automated checking and playback as well. Most DAWs can automatically convert captured MIDI performances into notation.

On the other hand, some advantages of handwritten work discussed earlier in terms of working in song journals apply to music notation as well. Sensory and tactile aspects of hand notation can change how and what you hear, and thus what you can conceive and compose. Handwritten notation also encourages you to use less formal and partial notation formats, and to interweave these freely with lyrics and related material. This can be helpful in earlier drafting stages, when you don't want to be slowed down by notation issues that don't serve the writing process at that point. (I recall one co-writing session with a composer mostly accustomed to musical theater writing, who simply could not proceed without preparing a rough sketch of a full piano accompaniment for each bar of the song.)

Because I do a lot of handwritten notation, I maintain separate journals for different kinds of notational work: e.g., journals with staff paper for writing instrumental tunes or arrangements, and journals with grid paper for chord diagrams. I also find loose-leaf pages helpful for notational sketches. When working at my instrument, particularly piano, it's nice to have a single fresh, separate page to work with. I keep draft pages in a single folder, roughly in chronological order. (I prefer to write on just *one* side of loose-leaf pages, so I can leaf through them later without flipping them, and to make copying easier. Yes, I know this wastes paper!)

- **Lead Sheets.** The many transcription decisions required in notating your song require you to concretize aspects and choices that might otherwise remain fuzzy. *Lead sheets* (single-line melody and lyrics, with chord symbols) can help you to work more structurally with your song, and to separate compositional from performance aspects, particularly in detailed revision and polishing. You can use the lead sheet to help problem spots such as repetitive melodic choices, range problems, and phrasing issues.

- **Chord Charts.** While *chord charts* (only chord symbols, no written notes) in particular are often prepared only in advance of a session, they offer significant value—not always sufficiently recognized—in earlier writing stages. Too often, musicians rely only on short chord sequences that they can easily play from memory, leading to simplistic progressions with lots of unvarying repetitions and loops. The simple act of writing down the chords in a separate chart allows you to think more structurally and narratively about the progression. You can annotate chords above lyrics, but to derive real compositional benefits, I strongly believe it is essential to *see* a progression's structure in its own separate notation. Working in a DAW can provide similar benefits, serving in effect as notation you can manipulate and vary, and circumventing limitations of your instrumental chops.

I am a vociferous advocate of songwriters learning and using alternative chart forms, such as the simple, self-transposing Nashville Number System (chords set as numerals representing scale degrees, rather than as letter names). As the name commemorates, these charts developed in Nashville studio environments and are familiar in country and related roots genres such as bluegrass. But the format can be used effectively in any genre with primarily diatonic chord changes and unambiguous tonality. An advantage of the Nashville Number System format is working in terms of harmonic function as you write out the progression.

Moving from Journal to Computer

I usually find there is a point where a song lyric has stabilized enough that writing out a new "fair copy" version in the journal becomes more chore than help. At that point, I switch to the computer and type in a clean lyric version to print. In co-writing, this often signals a point where we're ready to try a quick work demo and want a clean version to perform from. We may still continue marking up this printed version of the lyric. Once I hand-annotate a lyric sheet with suggested changes, that becomes an artifact I'll save as part of the song's archival trail.

A WORKING EXAMPLE

Recently, I attended the wedding of two former students, Eden Forman and Lukas Pool. (They met, in fact, in my old-time music ensemble.) Months earlier, thinking ahead to their wedding, I had jotted down a lyric seed, with a possible song-as-gift in mind (the references to their names being the conceit of the lines): "In Eden's garden, a pool well hidden." This quickly became:

> *Deep within Eden's garden*
> *Under shaded boughs well hidden*
> *Lies a quiet leaf-shadowed pool*

(This exemplifies, by the way, why a seed with a specific timeline or purpose belongs on a project seed list, or at least a "Seeds for Current Projects" or "Urgent Seeds" list. If I hoped to write the song in time for the wedding, throwing it into Seeds

Central wasn't going to work! Creative workflow management and task management work hand in hand.)

After the ceremony, I was sitting with other guests around a campfire. A new pine log was thrown on the fire, flaring up fiercely. "Don't worry," someone said. "It's pine; it will burn down soon." Songwriter me: "Hmm . . . some love is like that. . . ." I quickly thumb-scribed a seed, then a sketch, by the pale light of my phone.

Here are three of the left page/right page spreads from journal pages I wrote, working with the seed the next morning. In this case, I transferred material from my digital notes *back* to my handwritten journal, in order to develop the song. You can see many of the elements discussed in this chapter (and later chapters) in use here.

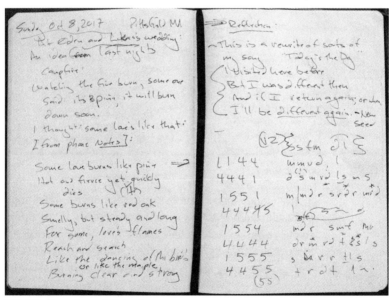

FIG. 5.2. Song Journal Entry 1

I noted the date, location, and context, and a first entry for what is in effect a song log. (Note that a pre-printed page number is part of the format of this particular journal. After experimenting with this format, I discovered that I actually prefer the clerical work of writing my own page numbers.)

I used the left page/right page layout (described in chapter 10) for reflections, connecting this song to an earlier song of mine. That recollection led to a different seed (later "rescued" and recopied to my journal end pages). I also used the facing page for side-by-side work with the lyric: chord chart (Nashville Number format), and melodic sketches (done in "solfege shorthand").

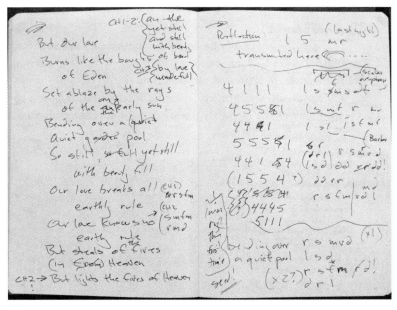

FIG. 5.3. Song Journal Entry 2

The next page spread shows a number of the other tools discussed: alternatives, cross-outs, carryovers, or bring-alongs (e.g., "our love breaks" to "our love knows"), annotations (e.g., "?" and "!" marks on the chords), song form markers (CH1, CH1-2), and even another new seed ("I was right the first time"—also rescued).

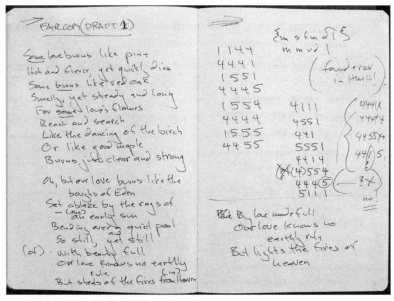

FIG. 5.4. Song Journal Entry 3

The third page spread shows an important step in drafting: recopying fragments from the earlier sketches to a first "fair copy" draft. Underlined syllables are reminders of the phrasing desired. Some alternatives considered live on as variations for first and second choruses.

Many of these techniques are integrally connected to my *handwritten, black-pen, bound-journal* working style. To preserve this information while typing lyrics into a digital file would be difficult, and would likely break rather than facilitate the flow of the work.

Eden and Lukas, I still owe you the song! In the meantime, congratulations again. As a preliminary wedding present, I've made this example out of you.

YOUR JOURNAL ARCHIVE

Everything about my approach to song journals reflects a willingness to keep ancillary materials *visible* and *permanent*. To work this way requires an odd mix of attitudes: egotism— ratcheted to a level that would surely appear to some observers a kind of monomania—combined with a casual disregard for the level of polish or completion of any particular material. A messy encyclopedism is what you're after: confidence in your *working*, humility about your *work*.

You want to be completely comfortable spilling ideas, sentences, and phrases onto paper—turning the fleeting and ephemeral to artifact and archive. You need the presumptuous belief that there is value in maintaining that record of search and discard. You show your love for the creating as much as the creation, when you honor and care for your journal archive.

FIG. 5.5. The Author's Song Journal Archive

CHAPTER 6

Song Revision and Critique

Just as sketches get turned into more complete drafts, drafts in turn progress via *revision*. In sketching, you need not account for every stray idea captured. Once you have a draft, though, you want to manage workflow more carefully, as material flows (or doesn't) into each successive version. There are two main reasons for this extra care: making sure potentially useful material isn't lost track of and left, for practical purposes, irretrievable; and removing irritants that can slow your forward momentum.

Some revision work will reflect your private development activity. But eventually you are likely to get external critique on the song, which will in turn generate other kinds of material, such as comments and suggestions, that need to be managed and linked to song materials. Managing critique as a *separate* process from revision is, in fact, essential to the integrity of both processes. Just as you learn to catch song seeds without immediately "working" them, there are specific skills involved in capturing *information* from critique without feeling compelled to immediately translate this into a decision about revising the song. Thus, these two workflow streams are separate, but interdependent.

MANAGING SONG REVISIONS

Much of revision is taking away. Michelangelo famously described the art of sculpture as removing marble until the form emerged. We songwriters, though, must first make the marble, then carve. Thereafter, it is not just by accident but by intention that we need to throw a lot away. This is a sign our process is working *well*. I tell aspiring writers to aim to write five to ten times *more* material in sketches and drafts than they know there is room for in the song.

They will thus be under no illusions that a given line should stay in the song, just because they wrote it on the page while working on the song.

But this raises two central questions for managing the workflow of revision.

1. How many versions should you save? You can spend a lot of time revising a song—in fact, if you're not careful, you can revise almost endlessly, and wind up chasing yourself in circles! A more disciplined approach to revision involves structuring the revision process itself, into a succession of modified drafts and more formal *versions*.

2. What happens to all that thrown-away material? It's helpful to think in terms of a few types of "containers" that can help manage the workflow of revision in a seamless way, and that accommodate different working styles. Each of these containers is a place to put material *not* carried forward into the next draft version. Because sometimes, we hang on to the marble for our next David.

Successive Versions and Snapshots

In the days when my first draft of every song was in a handwritten journal, I trained myself to write successive versions in those permanent pages, and not to worry about wasting paper or space. I felt it was worth it, in the end, to have a trace of the process of writing the song. Often, that act of recopying the lyric forward onto new pages—a sort of preliminary "fair copy" of the work in progress—was where the most significant insights came.

If you are working in a handwritten song journal, when you are ready to make a new revision of a song, go to a new page and copy only what you need into that version. Anything not carried forward remains available on the preceding pages. (Working by hand in a loose-leaf page format, you can't count on the chronology the bound journal provides, so label your previous draft, and number and staple the pages.)

Additional care is needed when you work in a mixed digital and paper environment. In my paper archive, I keep one clean printout matching each digital snapshot version. This is partly for redundancy—because you never know! (This brings up the huge topic of making security backups of your material, discussed in chapter 9.) I also save any printout that I have annotated by hand. Beyond that, I've found that it's good practice to get rid of stray extra copies, such as copies made for a critique session, with no written comments.

Shifting Formats

Certain work stages and "next creative steps" are facilitated by working between physical and digital forms. I often print out a clean, typeset lyric sheet, then add side notations for melody, chords, revision notes, etc. Eventually, I flow those annotations into an updated digital format, such as a chord chart, lead sheet, or audio recording. I may still save that hand-annotated material, even if I have faithfully transcribed all annotations, and even if, in that process, I've consolidated and further revised the handwritten material. I treat printed material, once marked up with changes, comments, alternatives, or notes from a co-writing session, as an artifact with unique process information and value. So, I date and further annotate the pages to make clear the work *has* been transcribed, then save them in the physical folder for the song as part of the permanent archive.

Version Numbering

For digital versions of lyric sheets, lead sheets, or demos, I use just the song title as the file name for the most current version. When I'm going to make a significant new version, I first copy the current version and rename it with the latest version number. In the "live" or current file, I bump up the version number in the file, and record the date of the revision, but leave the version number out of the file name. The file without a version number in the name should always reflect the current version.

Working primarily in a digital environment requires additional housekeeping. When you decide a new "snapshot" version is warranted, I suggest the following steps:

1. Rename the old version <SONG NAME>-Version n.

2. Make a new file with just the song name as the title.

3. In that new song file, add a note incrementing the current version number.

With this protocol, your new version doesn't clobber the old version. Instead, you wind up with a series of version files numbered V1, V2, V3, etc., with the current version always the file *without* a version number in the title. For example, if you were working on "Break My Heart" version 3, and now are creating a new version, rename the old file "Break My Heart-V3," and the now-current version just "Break My Heart." (Believe me, this is better than "Break My Heart-FINAL," "Break My Heart-REAL FINAL FOR SURE," etc.) In the current version file, update the annotation, e.g., from "Version 3" to "Version 4." Also include the date of the last—even minor—update (I don't like to depend on date stamps of computer files). I also carry forward the date of the first relatively complete draft of the work, so that I can trace it by that date in handwritten journals.

If you work this way, you also don't need to actively delete material. As you create each successive version, provided you hang on to the earlier version, you can delete away to your heart's content. Any material that isn't diverted into an alternative flow as discussed below—into your Parking Lot, or Stewpot, or saved off as new seeds—remains in an archived earlier version. There is always a chance you may later want to revisit a decision to delete material. Your version history serves as your trail of breadcrumbs.

How Many Versions?

How many versions should you save? There is no universal best practice here. In general, I save snapshots of versions corresponding with each successive demo version for a song, as well as starting and ending versions for co-write sessions, and versions brought into critique sessions. I also distinguish between substantive rewrites that change a song's overall structure or point of view, and more detailed "polishing" revisions that might involve adjusting a few words here or there. It is a good learning experience to take a few of your songs and do a thorough "stop-motion" series of snapshots, if only to gain appreciation for the many rounds of revision that a song can go through.

Otherwise, with good workflow practices for "rescuing" material out of older versions, you can find a comfortable level of "songkeeping" detail that matches your working style, and your interest in the process. As we move from version to version, a key aspect of this workflow practice involves setting up the right containers for sifting material out of individual versions that we may want to handle separately, or in a different way. In the next few sections, we discuss a set of such containers that work well in coordination.

The Parking Lot

The *Parking Lot* is a tool used by many workshop leaders and facilitators: a place for things you commit to dealing with eventually, just not right now. This is highly applicable to songwriting's non-linear process, especially since we often change song structure itself considerably from version to version. As a result, in the course of revision you are often handling scraps and fragments generated for the song, which you are fairly sure will ultimately belong in the song you're working on. You're just not yet sure *where*.

For example: you start a song with one verse and a chorus. An idea for another verse pops into your head. You're not yet sure if it will be the first, second, or third verse. You could write it directly into the draft; that means either making a preemptive decision about its placement, or weakening the connection of the page to the song structure. Or, you can park it in your Parking Lot.

Your Parking Lot should remain readily accessible during work on the song, both to keep adding to it and to quickly scan it for the right material for a new context. Having it as a separate file allows you to keep it ready at hand without visually clouding your perception of the song form as it emerges on the page, and without losing track of it by "parking" it at the bottom of the draft. A parking lot is *non-sequential* in its own structure. You might add stuff to it from any spot in the song, and that material, if used, could wind up anywhere in the song.

The Stewpot

It's also useful to have a separate container for material you have now decided is *not* likely to be used in the song at hand (again, for which it was originally generated), but which you believe or suspect might be useful elsewhere, either for another song or in another context more generally. I call this container my *Stewpot*. (You may have your own name for it; for example, songwriter Danny Carnahan calls it his "fragment file.")

Your Stewpot is not a container specific to *this* song or working session. Rather, it's a resource you will add to, and potentially draw from, in different writing sessions. In this regard, the stewpot is comparable to one of your seed lists. And, like song seeds, material you lift out of the song and banish to (well, squirrel away in) your Stewpot can be of any type (lyric, music, etc.). Consistent with our stewpot metaphor, let's call these fragments *morsels*.

Managing Morsels

A fair question is whether the morsels we pull from a song in revision need to be handled differently than song seeds. Can't we simply pull them out and put them in Seeds Central? This practice would, however, dilute the power of the seed list, due to some important workflow distinctions between morsels and song seeds:

- A song seed is a fragment that strikes you, at the first, as a song-worthy bit of material, that could serve as a starting point for a song (even if not a title or hook). In contrast, a morsel might be a larger fragment, such as a rhymed couplet or entire verse or other section, a musical interlude too busy for the final song, or a compound of several facets (e.g., lyrics and music) already fused. (It's easiest to "morselize" lyric material, trickier perhaps to work this way with notation—chord charts, lead sheets—or audio files.)

- When we capture a song seed, we take pains to strip distracting source context from it. A morsel, on the other hand, is material you created in response to the song draft at hand. It is likely to be entangled with that thematic and structural context, and will probably not "lift out" nearly as cleanly as a song seed would. To use that morsel in a different song, those messy bits of embedded context will need to be untangled. You'll have some deconstruction (or let's say "mastication") work to do. But you don't want to take time to do that when you first throw it in the Stewpot.

- Song seeds are usually very small fragments. A morsel can be a fairly large chunk of material. Suppose you quickly jam on a number of verses for a verse-refrain song, then pick the strongest four or five for the final song. Where do the other verses go? They might constitute one big morsel in your Stewpot. You might eventually split them up, strip the first song's refrain out, or pull a single seed from the material, but this is not work you want to do, or can do, in the act of discarding it from the song at hand.

Your ongoing Stewpot will form a series of "panels," with material drawn from various songs, related material left contiguous, and some sort of separator between chunks. It isn't usually essential to note the song from whence the morsel cometh. Since you've decided it doesn't work in that original context, in order to use this material you'll need to tease out, eliminate, or recast those thematic or content links anyway.

Sometimes, you must remove a substantive chunk of material that hangs together as a unit. In fact, it's not uncommon to discover you have actually been writing *two* interleaved songs, when you thought you were writing just one! (I have seen this so often in coaching student writers through revisions that I jokingly call this operation "song mitosis.") In this case, you might shortcut the Stewpot and directly create a new sketch or draft for the excised material, as a now-separate song.

Example Morsels

Returning to my earlier "Crazy Good" song example: Sally and I both loved the "penguin" line. (I'd just seen and been deeply moved by the movie *March of the Penguins*.) But, having spent more time in the South, Sally also knew how well our intended audience (given our genre) was likely to relate—not!—to that image. We also loved the quirky specificity of "your old friend Joe," and thought it might be stronger instead to say a little more about him. So we kept the "snow" rhyme—but stayed with our friend Joe for the winter:

There's crazy like a taxi driver
Crazy like your old friend Joe
Putting up his Christmas lights
And waiting for the Georgia snow

So, what becomes of: *"Crazy like a [daddy] penguin / Keeping an [\his] egg warm in the snow"*? As written, it's a morsel, not a seed. For one thing, "crazy" is a link back to the context and frame of the song of origin. I could reduce it to a seed, but now is not the time to do that. So it becomes a morsel, and waits there in my

Stewpot. Sometime in the future, that penguin may come back as an unexpected guest. But it didn't make it into *this* song. Keep an eye out for your penguin lines, and remember: penguins are hardy creatures, who can survive a long time without nourishment. (NOTE: Since this morsel comes from a co-write, I also need to consider whether it is part of my co-write "session business" with Sally. These workflow considerations for co-writing are discussed in chapter 7.)

A well-known "Stewpot" moment in contemporary songwriting can be heard in the Beatles' "A Day in the Life" on the *Sgt. Pepper's* album. The entire middle bridge section, beginning with "Woke up, fell out of bed," was apparently a separate song or song fragment that Paul McCartney had been working on, that eventually found its way into the song. Here, the size of the fragment and its stylistic dissimilarity to the surrounding context of the final song was used to create sectional contrast and an ironic shift in tone.

The Usefulness of the Stewpot

Often a morsel is an unwieldy chunk, messily entwined with its originating song context. Hanging on to such material may seem like a lot of work, for somewhat uncertain creative value. It may seem like the point is to salvage potentially strong, but extraneous, material. Often, very strong material winds up in your Stewpot. In fact, sometimes it doesn't fit in the song *because* it's a strong line—perhaps too strong for its position in the song, where it can become a competing hook, title, or metaphor. However, I'll go further and claim the Stewpot is a useful—nay, invaluable—tool, *even if you never pull any material from it later!* Why?

Skilled songwriters must be "ruthless revisers," as songwriter Kathy Hussey puts it. You ask not just, "Is this a strong line?" but, "Is this a strong line *for this song*?" If not, you *must* be ready to lift that material out of the song. But if your only "working space" is the song draft itself, then the only place to toss discarded material is—away. And if you sense this material is strong in its own right, this is (and should be) painful.

I don't know about you, but whenever I write, two songwriter selves spar in my tortured soul. Practical, Mature Songwriter Me will eventually realize those fifteen ridiculous but oh-so-clever rhymes are really not helping the song. Vain, Egotistical, Childish Songwriter Me is convinced every line I write is precious—a legacy I am bequeathing to that ghostly crew, my Future Biographers. I need a little help to, as writing coaches like to say, "kill my darlings."

My Stewpot is thus mostly a "head fake": "Oh, I'm not *losing* that line. I'm just not *using* that line here, in this song."[3] This encourages me to be a ruthless reviser. It provides a liminal place for the rejected but not discarded, the gone (for now) but not forgotten. I am willing to banish my darlings—the killer lines I must kill—from *this song* because I tell myself they may yet see the light of day in some other song. I can thus be braver, bolder, more focused in excising inessential or distracting material.

The Stewpot thus does its most important work by emboldening me to remove material, to make the song at hand as strong and lean as it can be. It is a secondary benefit if I ever use that discarded material.

This points up a key distinction in workflow between your Stewpot and seed lists. Song seeds are material you *initially* note as interesting and potentially song-worthy; they are by definition, then, worth at least a second glance. This is why the Appointments with Inspiration described in chapter 4 are essential to integrating song seed catching into your creative practice.

Stewpot morsels are not vetted to the same degree. We know they don't belong in the current song; we only suspect they might be useful elsewhere. The Stewpot's effectiveness as a workflow tool does not depend on our routinely reviewing it. Nonetheless, you can always add an appointment with your Stewpot as another background creative task for those low-energy puttering days. My songwriter pal Danny Carnahan, for example, regularly pulls out his Fragment File, scatters it around him on the floor, and sees if something sparks an idea.

What *is* essential for the efficacy of your Stewpot as a workflow practice is being discriminating about what goes into it. Not *every* rejected fragment goes into the Stewpot. Alternatives you are still undecided about should go in the Parking Lot. You can let

---

3. I owe the metaphorical use of the "head fake" as a teaching technique—which I have adapted here to creative self-deception via the Stewpot—to the late Randy Pausch, as he describes in his YouTube video that was later published as *The Last Lecture (Hyperion, 2008).*

go of removed material that isn't memorable and independently intriguing. Strike your own balance between clinginess and parsimony. Only what still has "juice" for you, and is likely to be of use to you, deserves a Stewpot's chance at reincarnation.

New Seeds

As discussed earlier, you can catch seeds in the midst of any foreground task, including creative tasks like writing a song. In fact, seed "sparks" and "cascades" (to thoroughly mix metaphors) become more likely as your songwriter's mind relaxes and starts free-associating, moving between focused and peripheral attention. Having practiced recognizing seeds provides a foundation for a subtle but potent workflow victory here. You feel less compelled to shoehorn them into the song. Unlike morsels for your Stewpot, these should be fairly separate, stand-alone ideas.

Happily, you can use many of the same mechanisms for capturing and handling this material as other seeds, with the one adjustment that you want to disrupt the flow of your foreground creative work as little as possible. You can jot them on the page or on song seed back pages in your journal, or on the computer in a separate seed notes file. One main consideration: will you care later that the seed was generated as part of this song or session? For example, was it a product of collaborative interaction in a co-write session? That will shape the details of your housekeeping practices.

Cleaning Up—and the Wastebasket

As you are finishing working on a song, it's good cleanup practice to cull through your Parking Lot. You'll either flow that material back into the song somewhere, pass it on to the Stewpot, or let it go.

Finally, yes, you can actually get rid of material. In fact, this is one rare moment in your creative workflow where you might need, or want, to actively *delete* material. The only reason to save *everything* is to have a full process history for your song. It is highly instructive to do this a few times, for a few songs. But if you do it for every song, you'll drive yourself, your co-writers, and likely a spouse or partner crazy!

If you don't anticipate a creative use for the material, and you're not making a snapshot of the process for later reflection, there can be a power in *throwing stuff away*. If you have a floor full of handwritten drafts, it may be satisfying to purge, arranging the versions you care about retaining. If you are working in a digital environment, you may not have the same visible evidence, and irritants, of leftover fragments and scraps. But it is probably a good idea to make clean decisions even about digital files. Lurking versions invite confusion later on, when you come back to a folder without all the context that is fresh in your mind at the moment. And having a ritual of cleaning up after a song can release some psychic energy as well.

Song Logs

For a song that goes through multiple revisions, it is helpful to maintain a separate "log" file listing successive versions and revisions, with main changes made and why. You can also use your song log to capture notes, lessons learned, rationale for revision decisions, and any interesting anecdotes about the writing process you'll want for your "The Making of . . . " *Rolling Stone* interview.

The workflow diagram shown in figure 6.1 summarizes the various work products and activities discussed in this chapter and the last.

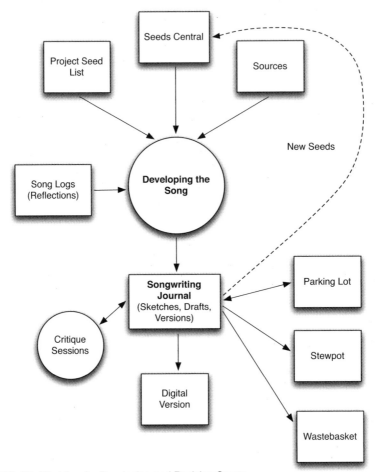

FIG. 6.1. Workflow for Developing and Revising Songs

MANAGING SONG CRITIQUE

Critique is essential to any creative work. It can come in many forms, and be sought out or encountered, at many stages of song development. There is almost as much to learn about the critique process as about the writing process itself. I have developed my own approach to facilitating song critique, both as a writer and co-writer myself, and as a teacher.

As with the generative phase of catching ideas, and the creative work of making sketches and drafts, some workflow aspects of managing critique are worthy of attention in their own right. The good news: from a workflow standpoint, once you have systems set up for sketches, drafts, and revisions, you have much of the housekeeping needed to also manage the wealth of information that comes at you in the context of critique. You will need just a few adjustments and extensions that reflect the role of critique within the songwriting process, and the nature of the resulting materials and work products.

Where does critique occur in the songwriting process?

An oft-bandied-about maxim concerning creative work is that one should separate out generative from evaluative and editorial phases. It is the case that, in rapid sketching for example, your goal is to stay in flow, to generate alternatives without second-guessing and revising on the flow. Yet even in such intuitive, internal solo creative work, there are inevitably quick loops of generative *and* editorial activity, as you evaluate those alternatives and select the best options for the song. In contrast, activities usefully designated as critique have specific characteristics:

- Generally, we critique work that is, if not complete, at least at some stable stage of work in progress. When putting together a first version of a song, I don't call it critique every time I jot down a line, decide I hate it, and keep looking for a better line. Thus, integrating critique into your creative workflow relies on a good system for managing snapshot versions and revisions, as discussed. In fact, one important reason to make a snapshot version is in preparation for a critique session.

- Critique does not imply *only* criticism—that is, negative criticism. Many critique protocols begin with very open-ended questions: What is working, *and* what is not working, in the song? Some protocols begin explicitly with a round of positive affirmations before moving to more "critical" comments. And it's just as important to track positive responses to your song as it is problem spots and suggested changes. Knowing where listeners hear "golden moments" can guide many later decisions.

- Just as it is often helpful to separate generative from evaluative work, in critique, it's essential to separate *evaluative* work from *revision decisions*. Observations and suggestions made in critique are contingent—they are not yet changes you have committed to.

A typical process error inexperienced songwriters make in receiving and processing critique is to try to respond to each comment with an immediate decision about what to change in the song. This can lead to resistance to input and suggestions, or to losing control of your own song by being *too* responsive to those suggestions—suggestions that may be misguided or might introduce other problems.

This means you need ways to record critique comments neutrally, then later work through those comments and fold considered responses into the next revision. In workflow terms, you need a separate "container" for the information gleaned during critique. Though this critique log might *look like* a series of revisions, it is entirely different in terms of workflow—it is information, not decisions.

- In critique, listeners generally listen to the *whole song*, then comment. Although there are different protocols for commenting, the process as a whole allows for—in fact, encourages—comments that are *non-sequential* with respect to the song's structure. You rarely ask for critique on the first verse, then the chorus, then the second verse, etc. At the same time, many critique comments do address localized spots: particular words or phrases, specific chords in the progression, etc. In fact, one skill in giving critique is learning to focus initially broad and sweeping comments to more localized and specific observations, and good critique facilitators know how to coach critique givers in these directions. Other critique comments may be more global, yet may deal with specific aspects of the song. You need ways to record critique that can handle this diversity of non-sequential yet highly localized comments, as well as a multitude of more general comments.

- Critique is often done in a *collaborative* setting: a peer songwriter circle, or an open workshop with a panel of experienced songwriters, publishers, producers, etc.

That means critique comments come out of a group interaction. One comment may spark others; some comments might directly conflict.

Preparing for Critique

When preparing a song for a critique setting, settle on a "best version so far," that you are ready to bring to that setting. If you have changes you intend to make but haven't generated an up-to-date version reflecting those changes, that is a problematic time to solicit external critique. This might seem obvious, yet it is striking how many times songwriters bring in work, and as the comments start flying, counter almost every point with, "Well, I know about that, and I was meaning to change that line. I just haven't got around to that yet. . . . " Your critique log should sit between two clear snapshot versions of the song, like alternating beads on a necklace. (The critique beads are the ones made out of sharks' teeth.)

That doesn't mean you can't critique an incomplete song or work in progress. I've led rich and rewarding critique sessions looking at just chord progressions, or single verse-chorus sections. It is useful, though, to prepare a summary of the current state of progress of the song, to indicate stubs for sections planned but not written yet, etc.

Print lyrics (and, if appropriate, chord charts or lead sheets for critique on music) to share with everyone in the group who will offer critique. Include a version number and date. If you get an annotated copy and come back to it much later, you'll want to know which version was critiqued. Some people are more comfortable jotting down notes on a physical sheet. They might write down things they aren't comfortable saying, or don't get a chance to say, out loud. You can leave critique-givers' names on the sheet optional, but do let them know you'll collect the sheets at the end of the session. It's good *not* to leave extra copies floating around.

Receiving Critique

Most songwriters drastically underestimate how much information can come at them, quickly, during a critique session, and drastically *over*-estimate their ability to retain it and retrieve it later. It's not unusual to have a dozen or more points to keep track of, and because not all of these will be localized, you can't use a later tour through the song as a sort of "memory palace" to retrieve points made. You genuinely need some explicit kind of annotation.

In addition, remember that you are not in the calmest state of mind when receiving critique. It's your song—your baby! You will be reacting emotionally to some challenging comments, dealing with adrenaline, fight-or-flight reflexes, nervousness, vulnerability, defensiveness, and your valiant efforts to quell them—all the while trying to act like a minutes-taker at a board meeting. In this situation, the mere act of dutifully *transcribing* the comments can be immensely grounding. (If you are really unable to do so, you can appoint a friendly scribe to do the honors.)

Record the critique discussion if possible. (This is particularly important to share and process critique later with a co-writer.) But don't let the fact that you're recording be an excuse not to also take written notes. Try to write down each verbal comment, whether or not you agree with it, and even if you get conflicting reactions from different listeners. You can use a master "fair copy" of the lyric/lead sheet, etc., for capturing localized comments, and a separate critique *log* for capturing more general and global comments.

Processing Critique

At the end of the session, collect all the individual copies you provided to the critique group. Eventually, you can transcribe and consolidate these written comments onto the work products where you captured discussion comments. These materials are brought into your next working session for actively revising the song. For a co-written song, be prepared to share this critique information with your co-writer(s), even (especially) if they were not present at the critique session.

When you're ready to do a next revision, I suggest that you review and respond, *in all the ways you choose to respond*, to specific feedback and critique received in that critique session, and to reflections and insights sparked by reviewing that feedback. Snapshot this version, before you do further work on the song. If you can, share this version with the group that provided the feedback. It will be energizing for them to hear how their feedback made a difference and helped in your further developing the song. A song circle of peer writers might even design such reporting back as a regular practice of the group.

CHAPTER 7

Co-Writing and Collaboration

Co-writing and collaboration skills are essential for songwriters, in every genre and market of today's rapidly evolving music industry. Of the many books about songwriting craft, few discuss the specific skills and practices required for co-writing or collaboration in detail. The topic deserves a book of its own (yes, another one!). Here, we will focus on ways co-writing and collaboration add additional challenges to the "songkeeping" practices and tools discussed so far.

The ability to co-write—confidently, effectively, responsively, and innovatively—demands not only intensified songwriting chops, but also distinct professional, process, and relationship management skills. These skills are sometimes put into action in situations where you write to tight deadlines and exacting project requirements. As new technologies and industry practices further reshape creative roles, team writing, virtual co-writing, and songwriting for diverse media (film, television, online) will demand new versatility and process flexibility from songwriters.

In the workflow management practices discussed so far in this book, I've suggested approaches that scale up, for writers with large catalogs and long-lasting professional careers. One reason to adopt practices that may seem very detailed for your more intuitive solo writing is to prepare for collaboration. Adopting more care in tracking versions and revisions is, in effect, becoming aware of ways you are "co-writing with yourself." As soon as you are involved in serious co-writing, all these workflow considerations intensify. The nonlinearity of the process, the need to manage small, incremental revisions (and check in with co-writers about them), the integration of micro-evaluations within drafts, and the ability to gracefully tolerate and track divergent possibilities and unsettled decisions all become essential skills of communication and collaborative decision-making. In addition, presenting as highly organized when working with co-writers will usually redound to your credit, while getting things wrong will suddenly shift from individual looseness to potential breakdowns in professional relationships.

Given all these factors, you'll be glad if your workflow management practices are a bit "overbuilt." A few caveats, though. Never show off your preparation as a badge of honor, or embarrass your co-writer if they didn't show up with a nice, orderly list of potential song seeds. Make your housekeeping as unobtrusive as possible to your partner, unless and until it proves useful in a session. And above all, never let the housekeeping get in the way of the creative work.

USING SEED MATERIAL FOR CO-WRITING

In chapter 4, "Supporting Practices for Seed Material," we discussed organizing seed lists for action. One important kind of "pre-work" is queuing up seeds to prepare for planned co-writing sessions, or as a spur to initiating new co-writes.

Preparing Seeds for Co-Writing Sessions

When you have a specific co-writing session scheduled, take time, if you can, to acquaint yourself with your partner's music before the session. Based on your impression of that writer's strengths, style, and interests, sift through your seed lists for strong candidates to bring to that co-write session.

Ideally, select several seeds of varying types (lyric title or phrase, idea or concept, melody, chord progression fragment, etc.). This helps you work responsively with co-writers who have different preferred working styles. If your co-writer is comfortable working music first, you can meet them in their comfort zone with a chord progression or melodic seed; conversely for lyrics-first writers, and so on. And having several seeds on hand demonstrates you're not adamant about working on any particular one. This is far more comfortable for your co-writer, who can say yes to a seed that interests them, but doesn't need to say a series of no's.

Whatever seeds you select, bring A-game material. You can hold back anything you want to write yourself, but you should have enough seeds that whatever you bring is something you consider strong, that has energy for you at this time, and that you think might interest that co-writer. Your guesses don't have to be right; simply showing up with a list selected in advance shows preparation and professionalism. Of course, you may not need to fall back on the seed candidates at all. Some co-writes get rolling right from the conversation in the room. Do not expect it, but welcome your co-writer arriving similarly prepared with starting seed ideas. (Maybe they'll have read this book too!) A nice protocol is to "audition" your respective ideas responsively.

Your "Seeds for Co-Writes" List

You can also work with seed lists in the complementary direction. If you are oriented toward co-writing, part of your regular review of seed lists should involve sifting out seeds you feel are promising, but where you're fairly sure you would not be able to write that song on your own. Think of this as your "Seeds for Songs I Know I'll Need to Co-Write with *Someone*" list.

In an Appointment with Inspiration (AWI), you scan your list until a seed "lands" for you, then write for a designated time. "Seeds for Co-Writes" are seeds you *don't* think you can develop on your own. But maintaining this list enables a different kind of Appointment; you review *this* list to nudge yourself to initiate new co-writes. You might have a particular co-writer in mind, or a co-writer with a particular skill set or stylistic bent. You can also scan this list in response to a particular pitch opportunity. If you find a promising idea and think of a co-writer you have already worked with, you are now in a position to suggest a co-write, with at least one starting seed idea and an opportunity to write toward. Or it might be a seed you just feel will require collaborative energy for you to develop.

These two practices are complementary. Let the co-writer lead you to the seeds. And let the seeds lead you to the co-writer.

In addition, some co-writes are initiated in response to a specific opportunity, available to one or both writers. Clarify any such project goals at the outset of the session, if known in advance, when you set up the session. You can now select seeds in advance with two filters: your co-writing partner, and the opportunity at hand. Similarly, you can preview candidate seeds from each partner at the session start, now filtered through the criteria of the project.

MANAGING THE CO-WRITING SESSION

Okay, so two (or three or four!) songwriters are off and running with a starting idea—maybe pulled from one of your "starter" seed lists, maybe an idea that just emerged in the room. What materials will you be working with?

Co-Writes in the Songwriting Journal

My general practice is to use my physical, bound songwriting journal in a co-writing session. I do not keep separate journals for solo and co-writing; I do designate co-write entries as such in the journal table of contents, along with all co-writers. On the session pages, I date the entry, note the location of the session, and list all co-writers (that is, everyone in the room who might wind up a potential co-writer).

The session begins as soon as we are interacting, not just once we have settled on a song idea. That is significant, because it means that all interactions in the room are potentially part of the co-write. If anything said by me or by one of my partners in the room seems like potential material—essentially, a seed—I faithfully write it *in the session pages*. My attitude is, if it got said aloud, it's on the table as potential shared material to develop.

There are some important exceptions to this principle of co-writer's etiquette. If it's a "show and tell" period where writers are simply sharing other work in progress, of course it's hands-off. If my co-writer says, "I've been working on an idea for a song about aliens landing at the mall," I don't immediately say, "Yeah, great idea! Let's write that one!" Nor do I silently scribble in my journal, leaving my co-writer worried. If I wonder whether I'm perhaps hearing a shy co-writer tentatively throwing an idea out for a reaction, I'll feel it out; but I won't presume.

I have written with writers who had a habit of writing down *everything* said in the room, in a seemingly indiscriminate way. Though I will never assume intentional malice, sloppiness of process around *what gets written down* does make me nervous: a month later, who will remember that a jotted-down line was from an already-written song? (In fact, it was just these kinds of experiences that helped hone my attention to the housekeeping aspects of songwriting and co-writing—this book's focus.)

Every once in a while, in the heat of co-writing battle (or play), my sparking associative brain spits out something I know is not relevant to the song at hand, and also not a line or phrase heard from my co-writer. It's mine—it just happened to "land" during the co-write. My rule of thumb here is: if my co-writer heard that line or phrase later, would they have any way of knowing that I thought of it while we were in the session together? If the answer is no—if it feels like a clean "outside idea," that isn't a great candidate for a later co-write, and might even disrupt the session if I toss it out there—I may unobtrusively flip my journal to the end pages and write down the seed there. (There, now you know my little secret—the next time you co-write with me, you can watch to make sure I don't "deal from the back of the journal"!)

Shared and Private Workspaces

When co-writing is in swing, it is helpful to have a *shared* document, visible to and ideally editable by both parties. If one party must act as de facto session scribe, they should be a faithful, impartial scribe, as willing to write down their partner's ideas as their own. In addition, each partner may be doing some writing in their own journal or loose pages, or on their computer. These two kinds of workspaces—shared and private—can affect the dynamics of the session in subtle yet profound ways. These also impose some workflow management tasks at the session's end.

Private workspace in a co-write session provides a safe zone where you can jot down material *not* immediately visible to your co-writer. This need not be for selfish or secretive purposes. Sometimes, private space such as my journal pages allows me to regulate the pace at which I throw out ideas—for example, if I sense my co-writer's pace is a little slower. If whatever I type is immediately seen, or else I must keep it in mind and trust short-term memory, I am forced to choose between breaking my own flow and potentially disrupting my partner's.

Be clear about whether what you write in a private-space area belongs "to the session" or remains your own material. You can use seed lists at the back of your journal to sift out material generated *in* the session, but in your estimation, not *of* the session.

Scan-and-Match in Co-Writing

In chapter 5, we described scan-and-match as an important technique for making use of your song seed lists in developing a song. As well as using a song seed as a focused starting point for a song, this technique allows you to draw on seed material at certain other junctures in the writing process. To use the technique effectively, you need your seed lists readily available. This is one of the main motivations for compiling and organizing seeds into your Seeds Central.

While seed scan-and-match is useful in solo writing, it really comes into its own in co-writing. At any point where there is draft material on the table, you can turn to seed lists to rapidly scan for suitable material. A typical spot for scan-and-match is when a top-line writer is listening to a track in a studio setting and looking for a possible melodic and/or lyrical hook that would match the feeling and flow of that track.

As in solo writing, you want to pick your moments carefully, and turn to seed lists not out of fear but in the spirit of playfulness, looking for surprising juxtapositions. Where appropriate, you can try out candidates with your co-writer. Here, because you are scanning and matching from a list, there is less pressure—on either of you—to accept a weak match. Your co-writer gets to say yes, not no.

Note that, to be effective, scan-and-match in co-writing involves a very different workflow than seeds pre-selected to bring into a session, one that depends on your having rapid and effective access to your Seeds Central. Co-writing situations present many challenges and high stakes: time constraints, pressures of working face-to-face with other writers, the non-linearity of the process, and the need to bring your strongest material to the room. Preparing for and maximizing chances for success in these situations is one of the highest-yield payoffs of all the patient work you've done of seed catching and compiling your Seeds Central.

Co-Writing Session Parking Lot

Chapters 5 and 6 introduced workflow tools used in developing individual songs, including seed lists, the Parking Lot, and the Stewpot. Each of these tools takes on slightly different aspects and functions in a co-writing context.

In any songwriting, whether solo or co-write, you are negotiating tensions between inspiration-based and task-based creative ideas. This tension surfaces strongly in co-writing, especially when there is a specific project goal in mind. Your co-writer(s) and you start working on a song idea. At some point, you check in: Are we on track? Have our concept and direction for the song drifted from what would be a good pitch for this artist or the needs of this project? *You need to be able to ask this question and have the answer be no, without breaking the energy of the session.*

To facilitate this flow, we can use a Parking Lot the scope of which is the co-write session itself, rather than just the song in progress. You say, "I'm loving where this song is going, and I want us to finish it. *But* I'm thinking it's not a great pitch for Artist X, and I don't want us to force it down that path. Let's put this sketch in our Parking Lot, take a fresh swing at a song idea for our pitch, and then maybe come back to this later." Or, if you are both more excited about that song and willing to let the project goal go for now, that's fine too. At least you are making that decision definitively and *collaboratively*, so the co-writing rapport is preserved. (Now, in a sense, it's the project goal that goes into the Parking Lot!)

Beyond material for immediate consideration later in the session, you also have the option of maintaining a separate Stewpot, or separate seed lists, for material generated with this partner. Whether this housekeeping is worth the trouble may depend on whether you have an ongoing writing partnership with that writer. For some of my long-term co-writers, I maintain not only lists of finished songs and works in progress, but also seeds for possible future development.

Other than these tools, many of the workflow tools and practices you need for co-writing are natural extensions of tools for managing sketches, drafts, and revisions in solo writing. One tool to consider, if co-writing work alternates between face-to-face and at-a-distance writing, is the "change tracking" annotation functionality offered by many editing tools and environments.

This functionality can be very useful when one partner makes a significant number of small revisions to a work product, and wants to aid their co-writer in reviewing and approving those changes. Such functionality was designed for applications like reviewing legal contracts, where every change makes a difference. Though not legal documents, songs are extremely compact works of art where even the smallest of changes—one word in a line, or one note—can make a big difference. Good co-writers manage the housekeeping so that everyone is on board and in consensus with the evolution of the song.

USING DRAFTS: OVER-THE-WALL CO-WRITING

In addition to bringing seeds into co-writing sessions, through pre-selected lists or via scan-and-match, you can also use co-writing to "activate" fragmentary song material such as sectional sketches and drafts. However, while you can bring an unfinished draft in to a co-write session, that can raise the issue of inviting a co-writer to work on material already in progress.

An alternative strategy I have used to initiate co-writes using drafts is by "over-the-wall" co-writing. I send a musical or lyrical sketch or draft to my co-writer via email or file sharing. They work on the section, at their own pace and inclination, then share results with me. If either of us isn't pleased with those specific results, we can always "disengage" that collaboration. I am left with my original lyric or music section, and the co-writer can work with whatever they generated if they desire, retargeting it to other work.

If we like the direction we're going, we can follow up with work done face-to-face, using video distance-collaboration tools—or even the trusty old phone call. "Live/at-a-distance" co-writing is sometimes difficult, because you lack the intimacy and proxemic cues (body language, shared physical workspace, etc.) of working in the same room. But if you can begin with a solid section of material that already reflects balanced collaborative effort, it is much easier to overcome these obstacles.

Over-the-wall co-writing can be an effective strategy, both with partners you've already written with and with new partners. It can enable you to engage with writers otherwise difficult to connect with, due to geography or schedule. Over-the-wall co-writing is a distinctly different process than live co-writing, whether face-to-face or remote. However, those very differences can aid writers less accustomed to the time pressures and other challenges of creating material live or "in the room" with another writer.

An ideal granularity for initiating over-the-wall co-writes, I find, is with one or two sections, preferably in just one facet (i.e., lyric only or music only). It should be a relatively complete and well-structured draft, rather than either a loose sketch or a polished (and therefore less changeable) final version. Although you can send just song seeds over the wall, I find that the first stages of working with seeds in co-writing are best done live, if not face to face. There are just too many possibilities, too many ways to pivot, especially with an open-ended title seed.

As it happens, I do a lot of writing "one facet first," i.e., writing a complete "dry lyric" for the multiple sections of an entire song before I write any music, or conversely, an entire chord progression with no lyric or even melody. So, I am quite comfortable sending this form of material to a co-writer. However, some co-writers find it very challenging to work this way. Therefore, a draft of just one or two sections is often the best starting point: more than a seed, already establishing structure, theme, and emotional focus, but still with plenty of room for the co-writing interchange to take things in a different direction.

If working primarily in a lyricist/composer division of roles (a little old-school now, but still used extensively in, for example, musical theater collaboration), it can be creatively rewarding to do over-the-wall co-writing as a swap or trade. In this strategy, each partner provides a section in their respective facet (lyrics, music), and hands it off to the other partner. You wind up, potentially, working on two songs in tandem, while also playing flexible process roles (e.g., both lyrics-first and lyrics-in-response-to-music, or vice versa).

If you are peer co-writers, each prepared to contribute to both lyrical and musical aspects, you can also swap sketches or drafts in the same facet. This latter way of working is a great complement to face-to-face peer co-writing. Often, a writer can work on both lyrics and music, but will be quicker or more comfortable at one or the other facet in live collaboration.

WRAPPING UP A SESSION

When finishing a co-writing session, it is good to allow time for some definitive "cleanup" activities, essential to managing workflow, decision-making, and next steps involving the session.

Review and assess the work you did during the session. What is the state of progress for each song worked on? What's your sense of the overall strength of the song as of now? What is the level of interest from each co-writer to continue?

Prepare a fair copy of the most current version of the lyrics, and a reference demo for as much of the music as you have completed. Include annotations of alternates, placeholders, lines you hope to beat, and stubs for sections still to be written. If you worked with both private and shared materials, make sure everyone leaves with one consistent set of shared materials. This serves as a snapshot of the state of the song, so that no one is relying only on memory when you return to those materials later. For one thing, you don't know *when* you'll get back to the song, despite everyone's best intentions. In addition, different writers' senses of what is settled and what is not can vary. Memories can change, and disagreements crop up easily. You might as well find out now! If you made starts or progress on multiple songs, acknowledge each of these.

In some genres, it is typical to agree on and sign a *split sheet* at the end of a co-writing or collaboration session, where you document each party's share of the collaboratively created work. There are legal considerations to these documents beyond our scope here, but in any case, it is certainly good practice not to let these questions be subject to the vagaries of later imperfect or wishful memory.

Clarify the next steps. If the song is not done, what's still left to do? Are there sections still to be written, or material flagged as provisional placeholders or "stuff to beat if we can"? What are the possible next creative steps?

Each writer might commit to specific activities to move the song forward, including an agreement that one or both of you might continue to work solo. ("Let's each take a stab at lyrics for those later verses. . . . ") But it is also good to establish a clear and shared understanding of what *won't* happen—e.g., that neither of you will work solo on the song before your next session. It might seem paradoxical to agree *not* to work on the song; but if one partner rushes ahead and finishes a song on their own, without an agreement in place, the other partner can be left feeling they were cut out of the loop. Even if they technically could "veto" changes in the now-completed draft, with too many new compositional decisions embedded, it may not feel like a co-write anymore—at least in those aspects *intended* to be collaborative. Compare this to a scenario where a composer sends music to a lyricist partner, fully understanding that co-writer will draft the lyrics on their own. The agreement is all.

I find it helpful to maintain a running "Co-Writes in Progress" list, to coordinate co-writing activity, especially when it involves multiple co-writers, working on projects at varying paces and degrees of urgency. I also may maintain a separate list for longer-term co-writing relationships, where we may have several active collaborations going. For each co-writer, I list each song we're working on and its state of progress—especially "open loops"—and any standing mutual expectations about next steps. Are we waiting for a next meeting? Or have we agreed it's okay to work on a new section independently and share the results at a distance?

A bad habit of mine (one I don't recommend emulating) is to let open loops languish and "die on the vine." I suggest that you periodically review co-writes in progress, and possibly move some songs, and even co-writer relationships, to a status of "Stale." This acknowledges the uncomfortable truth that some co-write attempts just don't engage the writers enough to warrant finishing them. You don't have to throw the song in the trash, or send a note saying, "I have cooled off on our relationship." Stale simply means it's not done, but my co-writer is not waiting for anything from me on this song, nor I them. Action has stopped; resuscitating the song will now require a fresh conversation. When stale co-writes linger on your purported "active" list, they can sap your energy, leaving you feeling guilty and eventually more likely to avoid the list altogether. It always hurts a bit, but when you remove "Guilt Co-Writes" from "Active Co-Writes," you maintain the energy of the list as a spur to action.

CO-WRITER LISTS

Over the course of your career, you will likely co-write with many people. A basic but important practice is to maintain up-to-date contact and publishing information for co-writers you have worked with or are working with. It is frustrating to have a good placement opportunity for a song that has languished for a while, and to suddenly realize you are out of touch with the co-writer, with out-of-date information on the lyric sheet, etc.

I have several "circles" in my co-writer registry. You will usually have regular co-writing partners you really like working with, whom you don't need an excuse to get together to write with. An ongoing partnership of this sort might be characterized by having several songs in progress, at different stages, at any particular time. Though it may duplicate some information on your "Co-Writes in Progress" list, I find it helpful to be able to survey at a glance the sub-catalog of songs completed with a given co-writer, and what (if anything) has happened with each of those songs. This should include finished songs that have not been recorded, cover recordings, and especially older songs you might otherwise lose track of, but could still be pitching or re-pitching.

You will also have a number of "one-off" co-writing sessions. These co-writes can sometimes produce strong work, but it is easy for these songs to get lost in the shuffle, and also easy to fall out of contact with these writers. Remember, though, that although you might co-write just once with someone, on an afternoon where you feel sluggish and unproductive, every co-write can potentially create a piece of intellectual property— a song—requiring ongoing maintenance and management in both your catalogs. Something may happen with that song years later. It's a bit like going on a speed date that might produce a kid—that night.

To maintain energy around closing open loops and keeping collaborations alive, some triaging and prioritizing is important. At the same time, it's also good to stay motivated and "hungry" to pursue new opportunities. So, it can also be useful to maintain a list of co-writers you *want* to write with. This should always be first and foremost because they are great songwriters in their own right and you love their work. You might be drawn to write with writers because your styles are very similar, or very different. While you can include "blue sky" dream co-writers, as in the co-writer "bucket list" discussed in chapter 10, this list provides best value by encouraging you to write down co-writers you might have access to, yet might not otherwise be bold enough to approach. Without being obnoxious, you can often find chances to make these co-writes happen—if you clarify the goal and dare to dream.

Co-writing and collaboration will become ever more integral in songwriting. New creative forms and rapidly evolving collaboration and distribution technologies will make collaboration, on the one hand, more seamless and immersive, while on the other hand (perhaps because of these innovations) making it more difficult to manage skillfully. Being able to manage the workflow of both your solo and collaborative songwriting work will be a critical skill set in this creative and professional environment. Managing solo work may at times feel like treating your own songwriting as collaboration of a sort—among various incarnations of "you" at different creative moments. In a complementary sense, managing collaborative workflow effectively will support those moments of magic when co-writing, at its best, feels like two or more minds creating as one.

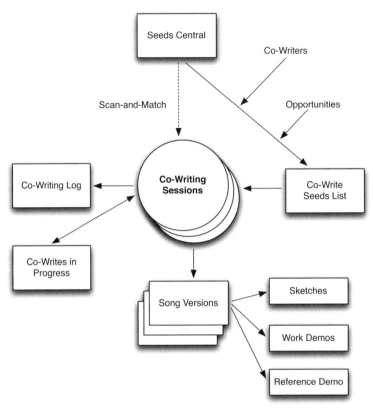

FIG. 7.1. Co-Writing Workflow

CHAPTER 8

Finalizing the Song

Working from a seed idea, and perhaps to a project or task requirement, we've produced drafts and snapshot versions of our song, sought out some critiques, and made revisions in response. We now, presumably, have a *complete, finished* song. Yay! What's next?

First: let's not presume. Often, we *tell ourselves* a song is finished when, in fact, many niggling little details lurk in scrawled notes on draft pages, markers on demo tracks, oddments of all the decisions we haven't quite—*settled* yet. Do we need "the" in the first line of the second verse? Is the last chord before the chorus a plain triad or a seventh chord? Before sending our new darling out into the world, we want to settle what we can.

A word to the wise: Once a song leaves your direct control, it will be subject to intense shearing forces from every side. Artists who cover the song, producers, engineers, session musicians will all bring their own ideas and tastes to the table. Some of this is inevitable, part of the process of an artist making a song their own in arrangement, production, and performance aspects. But if there is anything unique, innovative, distinctive, rule-breaking about your song that you *love* and believe in, you will have to fight for it. You do that best by being as clear as possible about every word, note, and chord in the song. That means cleaning up all the loose ends you can. If you can't always be *in*sistent, at least be *con*sistent. Any compositional decisions you leave fuzzy are invitations to mess with your song. Make sure everyone who hears your demo is at least clear about the way *you* hear it. Don't make them decide because you didn't.

Undealt-with details, even small ones, can also raise issues and cause conflicts with co-writers. I think this is because even minor snags in communications can erode confidence that decisions, at least *compositionally significant* ones, have been agreed on.

Otherwise, unilateral decisions can sneak in, whether by intent or by default, as the demo is cut for example. We want to make sure we're on the same page—and lyric sheet, and chord chart, and lead sheet!—with our co-writers. The best rule of thumb: if you are asking whether a given choice matters, it matters. If you don't decide, who will? And if not now, when?

FINALIZING THE LYRIC SHEET

Until now, lyric materials have helped in the work of writing the song and in collaboration. A finalized lyric sheet becomes a work product of additional documentary, and even legal, importance. Although technically, a composition is protected under copyright law as soon as it is committed to "fixed form," the finalized lyric sheet establishes that form more definitively. (In the unlikely event of litigation, earlier archival materials, such as dated journal pages, would also be valuable documentary evidence.) The lyric sheet is also an important vehicle for outreach to various other parties: artists, vocalists, musicians, studio personnel, other songwriters, fans, etc. In the next stages of preparing the song for recording, pitching, and release, a single reference point helps ensure consistency in all presentations of the song.

Fair Copy Lyric Sheet

The term "fair copy," dating from Elizabethan times or earlier, was originally understood in contrast to the lovely expression "foul papers": all the messy drafts of a manuscript, including author's revisions, cross-outs, marginal notes and comments, etc. The author (or someone else) would distill all these corrections and revisions into one clean manuscript, with all second thoughts, alternatives, or dubious lines resolved. This copy was "fair," as in beautiful and pristine, a neat handwritten draft that showed the form of the work in crystalline clarity. (I speculate it was also "fair" in the sense of just, conclusive, and definitive.) Implied also was that the fair copy was *in the author's hand*, making such documents of special editorial and archival importance. If it was the fair copy of a Shakespeare play, that really mattered!

Songwriters definitely produce their own "foul papers," as discussed in previous chapters. In one sense, each time you recopy lyrics from previous pages, clean up annotations and edits, or capture a current draft at the end of a co-write session, you make a temporary "fair copy." Still, preparing a *finalized* version is different. It is the fairest of copies, for you are now preparing the work for other hands, other ears. Making that an explicit step often leads to eleventh-hour edits that strikingly improve the work.

This stage is critical in co-writing. Though it's often helpful to work from a clean version during a session, preparing a fair copy at the end is an important separate step, even if it means exchanging materials after the session. Details that seemed incidental in the adrenaline rush of co-writing may have ripple effects and larger consequences worth resolving. And there's also something magical about saying, "So, that's our line?" to evoke that final round of editing that moves a pretty good line into a great line. Shared enthusiasm for this "finalization frisson" separates the pros from the schmoes. I love working with co-writers who match my energy for that final spit-and-syllable polish.

Formatting the Lyric Sheet

If creating your lyric sheet as a digital file, each application has conventions for saving backup copies, file names, etc. If you have been working in a collaborative environment where multiple authors make changes to the document, there is an advantage to shifting to a more *fixed* version for the final fair copy. I generally send lyrics as uneditable (e.g., PDF) files to any parties who will not (and should not) be altering lyrics, so the text doesn't stay a moving target. If you're using a change-tracking mechanism, this is the time to review and accept all changes. As mentioned in chapter 7, these are similar to the change-tracking tools editors use for managing drafts, and lawyers for "red-lining" contracts. Your final lyrics version is, in effect, a contract—with yourself as a solo writer, or with all your co-writers. This is *the* lyric—Version N, that is!

Titles

Song titles are funny things. A song's title is not the same thing as a hook or refrain within the lyric; it is not necessarily determined by the content of the song. It's true that a writer's inability to provide a title for their song is sometimes a revealing symptom of lack of focus or of a compelling central concept. But not every song needs an obvious title ringing out in the lyric; and conversely, not every refrain or hook needs to be, or ought to be, the title. Choosing the song's title is a *separate* decision. Thus, curiously, it's possible to finish a song and still not have quite settled on the title.

However, once the song is *done*, if you haven't yet, you *do* need to settle on that title! In fact, sometimes, it's only as you are preparing that final lyric sheet that the question really hits you. Now it's time to name the baby! This is as much a *marketing* as a compositional decision. Writing the song, craft dictates that you assume the listener will *not* hear the title first; you make the song do all its own work. But in finalizing the title, it's prudent to assume the listener *will* hear the title first—in effect, treating the title as an "advertisement" for the finished song.

That leads to a few considerations in choosing the title:

If there is narrative misdirection and a "reveal" in your song—a punch line or a twist—try to avoid a title that ruins a listener's *first experience* of the song. The George Jones classic "He Stopped Loving Her Today," written by Bobby Braddock and Curly Putman, has such a twist (I'll avoid a spoiler here), but the carefully ambiguous title doesn't spoil that "switcheroo"—the first time. Afterwards, the sly title increases the now clued-in listener's sense of being in on the secret.

Song titles do not have to be unique: titles alone cannot be protected by copyright, and so there can be many songs written to the same title. But be careful: duplicate names can cause confusion. Also, in a networked world, titles in effect become keywords. A more unique, distinctive, and memorable title not only will kindle more interest, but also will be easier to find on the Web and in copyright and licensing databases.

Every word, grammatical inflection, and even article in your title matters. When you alphabetize songs, consider especially the impact of articles at the start. Is it the "Song Title" or "The Song Title"? The "the" can make a difference!

Lately, there seems to be a trend for titles to include parenthetical clauses, which can come at the start or the end (or, I suppose, even in the middle) of the title. Sometimes they represent an additional refrain that is not the title of the song, but might be the familiar phrase listeners might search by. In some cases, I get the sense that the parenthetical titles are intended to invite listeners into a shared "community" around the song in a mysterious way. I'd be careful about them, and consider whether they represent a last bit of indecision.

In a more legal sense, copyright registration includes a field for *alternative titles*. These can be an insurance policy, making it more likely that an inexact search will yield a hit (not *that* kind of hit, sadly) on your song. Some songs are also released in multiple versions over time, with different titles used for different cover recordings or in different markets. (A translation of a song lyric into another language, on the other hand, generally results in a separately registered derivative work.) But again, alternative titles should not represent a *decision* you have not finalized.

Put the title (now that you've decided on it!) at the top of the first page of the lyric. It can be centered or left justified; personally, I like it to the left, along with the lines to follow. I also put the title in bold, in a slightly larger font than the lyric text (if that doesn't push the lyric to a second page). Make sure the title appears on any subsequent pages ("Story of My Life—p. 2"). Publishers' desks and studio control booths are as messy as songwriters' journals.

Copyright Notice

On a separate line after the title, put a *copyright notice*:

- © (Option-G in many editors), or just the word "Copyright."
- The year, your name, and publishing information—with the publishing company name immediately after your name, separated by a slash; then your performing rights organization (PRO) affiliation, in parentheses: e.g., Mark Simos/Devachan Music (BMI).
- The administration company info, if that's applicable.

Include the names and publishing information of all co-writers on the song, if available. (If I didn't get that information at the co-writing session, I find that a phone call or email to obtain the information is at least a nice check-in that we are finalizing song materials.)

There are different conventions used here. I prefer to keep publishing information contiguous with the writer's name when there are multiple writers, like this:

"My Cat Wants Breakfast"

© 2017 Mark Simos/Devachan Music (BMI), Desdemona Jones/Imaginary Music Publishing (ASCAP). All Rights Reserved.

(The optional period indicates the end of the writer list; it's not necessary with just one writer.) Especially when I am sharing lyrics in a public context, I usually add the phrase "All Rights Reserved," even though its legal force is now technically obsolete. If nothing else, it serves as an additional caution, in a media environment where lyrics in particular are difficult to protect.

Co-Writer Name Order

In general, there is no specific *legal* importance to the order in which writers' names appear in the copyright notice. Different percentages of ownership in the copyright, if any, need not be reflected in the name order.

If there was a clear division in creative roles, you can indicate: "Lyrics: William Shakespeare, Music: Johannes Brahms" (what a co-write *that* would have been!). But this does not reflect copyright ownership unless you write: "Lyrics © 2017 William Shakespeare, Music © 2017 Johannes Brahms." (Guess those lads still got game!) Even so, unless reflected in the actual copyright *registration*, this is a courtesy notification only, not a legally significant declaration. As co-writers, both parties share interest in the song *in its entirety*, as "tenants in common."

In most cases, then, the order in which co-writers are listed is presentational only, analogous to billing on a concert flyer. Yet songwriters can get persnickety about this. In settling an order for names, push can come to shove (and shove doesn't always lead to love—despite what Bonnie Hayes wrote in "Love Letter"). It can even turn into an odd pissing war as each writer swaps the order of names on *their* copy of the lyric sheet. If you can converse about it civilly, you can often apply a simple rule of thumb. The simplest and most objective is alphabetical order by last name. There may be a sense (not always shared) that one writer has moral right of precedence, perhaps if they brought in the starting idea, but this can get tricky. If one writer has more industry cachet, it may seem better for the team to list them first. And sometimes, one writer is the best reference for a particular pitch opportunity, or if the song will be pitched by that writer's publisher. Sometimes, it comes down to what no one wants to admit: if *you* are sending the song out, you want your name listed first. Since the order *doesn't* make a legal difference, there is the option of letting each co-writer manage their own version of the lyric and adjust publishing order as suits them. Make sure this doesn't create confusion and "orphaned" versions, for example, if later changes or revisions get made to the lyric that need to be reflected in both versions. In effect, these become alternate versions to be managed (see below).

Lyric Sheet Layout

There are varying conventions for lyric sheet layout that reflect personal preferences and also aid in different contexts of use. The following guidelines reflect my own practice, but are backed by some general rationale:

- Left justify lyrics. Skilled lyricists attend to all aspects of lyric structure, including line length. While songwriters measure lines in syllabic and rhythmic terms that do not always map directly to the visual length of the lines as text, it is still helpful to see lines laid out in a consistent way on the page. I find centered text to be a more "decorative" but distracting display. In physical or digital liner notes, or as part of your artist or songwriter Web presence, lay out lyrics with as much artistic license, centered text, Gothic and script fonts as you like.

- I prefer my lyrics to look fairly conversational. I capitalize the first words of each line, indenting only long carryover lines, without additional capitals.

  SOME PEOPLE TYPE THEIR LYRICS IN ALL CAPITAL LETTERS. I FEEL THE WRITER IS SHOUTING AT ME WHEN I READ LYRICS WRITTEN THAT WAY. DON'T YOU?

- How and where you break lyric lines can involve tradeoffs, and can also serve different purposes. While actively working on a song, you might break lyrics into shorter lines, for example, to keep track of matched internal rhymes. This might not be the best layout for a publisher to read while listening to the song (if they look at the lyrics as they listen; some won't, intentionally). For final lyrics, I try to have the layout reinforce structural alignment across parallel sections. On occasion, a "thought line" carried over to a new lyric line can be indicated with punctuation (as in the example lyric: *"Close our eyes and open them / Again— we read love's name in the candle's fire"*).

- Put a line break before chorus and bridge sections, and label them as such. You don't need to label verses. I italicize labels that precede written-out sections, and do put them in all caps (to set them apart from lyric text), followed by a colon, e.g., *"CHORUS:"*; then I indent that section enough that the first lyric line can start on the same line as the label. (If lines are very long, the label can sit on a line of its own.) I indent transitional sections such as pre-choruses, but rarely label these or separate them from the verse with a blank line. This applies also to sections following a chorus, such as hooks or post-choruses, typical of contemporary forms.

- If the lyric of a repeated chorus is unchanged, you can put the label *CHORUS* (without a colon) on a line by itself without copying the lyric, to more concisely indicate song form and sectional flow. Write the final chorus out in full if it fits on the page, or if there are minor wording changes or extensions such as a repeated last line or tag. If the lyric of a section (other than a verse) changes, you can number, and if necessary abbreviate, the labels, such as *CHORUS 1*, CHORUS 2, *PRE-CH 1*, or *PRE-CH 2*. This can help later in coordinating with lead sheets, and with tracking markers in studio session audio files.

Here's an example of my lyric sheet for "The Boughs of Eden," discussed in chapter 5. One annotation lives on in the fair copy: the "[it]" in the second line indicates a choice left up to the preference or interpretation of a vocalist or artist.

The Boughs of Eden

Version 1, 15 October 2017

> Some love burns like pine
> Hot and fierce, yet [it] quickly dies
> Some burns like red oak
> Smelly, yet steady and long
> For some, love's flames reach and search
> Like the dancing of the birch
> Or like good maple
> Burn just clear and strong

> *CHORUS:*   Oh, but our love
> Sways like the boughs of Eden
> Set ablaze by the rays of an early sun
> Bending over a quiet pool
> So still, yet still with beauty full
> Our love knows no earthly rule
> But steals of the fires of heaven

> As we gaze into the flame
> Close our eyes and open them
> Again—we read love's name in the candle's fire
> Dark blue heart, electrum's kiss
> Yellow-white, oh light of peace
> Surrounding brightness
> To you our souls aspire

> *INSTRUMENTAL CHORUS*

> *LAST CHORUS:*
> Oh, our love
> Sways like the boughs of Eden
> Set ablaze by the rays of the early sun
> Bending over a quiet pool
> So still, and still by love made full
> Our love knows no earthly rule
> But lights the fires of heaven

Spelling, Grammar, and Punctuation

Present your lyric sheet *professionally*, with correct spelling, punctuation, and grammar—at least to the extent that your lyric is actually grammatical! Your lyric sheet will potentially be seen by publishers, label A&R staff, and artists. Would you submit a résumé with misspellings and grammatical errors? With spelling- and grammar–checking tools readily available, there's no excuse for unintended mistakes.

Affected Effects

Some writers indulge in a kind of punk-chic orthographic style with lowercase letters ("what i said when she called") or numbers in the title. This can even show up in titles, such as the late Prince's "Nothing Compares 2 U," a major hit for Sinéad O'Connor. (I expect the "2 U" was carefully scripted, to match the desired vibe of the song. Of course, this was a song by an artist who, for a time, replaced his name with an unpronounceable graphic symbol.)

If you do use such orthographic special effects, make sure they appear intentional rather than accidental, and be consistent. (If this occurs in the title, this is a good situation to use alternate titles in registration.)

Periods

There are also differing conventions around concluding lyric lines with periods, like grammatical sentences. This format may help maintain consistency with lyrics in lead sheets, which in earlier conventions usually ended lines with periods. (In a lead sheet, staff systems may not break between lyric lines, so periods may provide additional guidance to singers.)

For me, ending lyric lines with periods is generally distracting on a lyric sheet. It implies a reading that insists on parsing the lyric into grammatical sentences, not always appropriate to the structure of song lyrics, which are *not* prose. Lyric format is closer to poetry on the page, but still distinct—in effect *transcribing* a form that ultimately lives as words *sung to music*. In *Songwriting Strategies*, I outline the distinction between lyric lines and *thought lines*, which approximate but are not identical to grammatical sentence boundaries. Thought lines may unfold across multiple lyric lines (through enjambment), or split a single lyric line into separate phrases. Just as often, lyrics as a whole unfold via sentence and phrase fragments.

Quotation Marks

Quotation marks are more troublesome. Quotation marks may help clarify when a song switches point of view or the lyric shifts to words spoken by a different character. One danger in using this notation is that: "You can't sing a quotation mark." (Yes, *I* said that.) As with titles that we expect to do narrative work for us, quotation marks may fool us into thinking a shift of voice will be obvious to the listener. With that caveat, for legibility's sake, I do tend to use quotation marks for individual lines, but may avoid them for an entire section that shifts into a different voice.

Alternative Lyric Sheet Formats

Unlike unresolved writing decisions annotated in drafts and revisions, there are legitimate reasons to maintain alternate formats of finalized song lyric sheets, in support of varying contexts of use. But it's critical to have a definitive finalized version, from which you generate these alternate versions and with which you keep them aligned.

Lyric + Arrangement

A lyric sheet used to evaluate song form and arrangement, or prepared for a demo session, might include labels for instrumental sections such as intros, outros (sometimes "midtros," if similar music occurs within the song), tags or turnarounds, solos, and fades. Some instrumental sections are structurally necessary, and may even have narrative importance. But often, such indications reflect that the lyric sheet is being used to document *arrangement* decisions, which can be subject to change by producers or artists. Similarly, a lyric sheet might or might not indicate vocal *ad libs* or multiple repetitions, depending on its use.

Phrasing Annotations

Sometimes when the phrasing of a lyric is subtle or very particular, I might add annotations: underlining the syllable falling on the first musical downbeat, or using spacers like "<>" to indicate lines that enter late or spaces (caesuras) within lines. These are essentially reminders for the writer(s) and/or cues or instructions for the vocalist; you may want to strip them out of more public versions of the lyric sheet.

Public Versions

Sometimes, you are in a position to post or distribute public versions of your lyrics, e.g., in hard copies handed out to fellow writers at song critiques. Have a version on hand without *all* the personal contact information you would want a publisher or producer to have.

Alternate Lines and Sections

Writers sometimes knowingly include "risky" lines in songs. You love the line; *you* think it works. But you acknowledge that line could be an issue—with your label if you are the artist, or with an A&R rep, producer, or artist if you're pitching the song.

Experienced writers and co-writing teams often write "defensively" in these situations, providing an alternative but keeping their preferred, if edgier, option in the lyric sheet. This is now not a decision *you* still need to make; it's one you are floating downstream. This can be a good place to use an alternate-line annotation (similar to those described for internal revisions) in a *final* fair copy lyric sheet. (Which version you list as primary, which as alternate—risky or safe foot first—is up to you. I'd have the primary option on the lyric sheet reflect what's on the demo, though.) Similarly, there are sometimes entire alternate sections in a song. Many pro writers, having been tagged enough times by publishers or producers to add a bridge to a "finished" song, learn to anticipate such later requests by writing an optional bridge up front and having it available "in the can."

Alternate Versions

Expanding beyond alternate words, lines, and sections, some songs may warrant full alternate versions—e.g. "gender-flipping" a song via some alterations of lyrics. From a workflow standpoint, one important distinction here is that you should probably keep alternate versions of the entire lyric sheet on hand, clearly labeled as such, as well as corresponding alternate demos. Many of these alternates will require a number of small changes throughout the song, rather than being localized to one spot.

In managing these alternate versions, all my suggestions here reflect a few general principles:

- *Manage your work products to maintain as much control as you can in what happens to your song downstream.* Anticipate the kinds of tug-of-wars that are likely to come up for your song; get out in front of those, if you can. For example, if you are pitching a song to an artist of different gender than the demo singer and current lyric, think through how *you* would alter your song for a different gender. Then at least *provide a lyric sheet with that version*—even without a separate demo. If you leave these editing choices up to the artist, I'll just say—*interesting* things can happen, such as reinterpretations of your song's meaning that might rub against your creative intention. And you might not find out till you hear the cut, at which point you are not going to stamp your foot and insist they pull the track!

- *If you write different, be definitively different.* If you are taking chances and doing innovative things in your song, and you believe in those innovations, it behooves you to communicate them as clearly and definitively as possible. Yes, the corners might still get knocked off your song in translation, but let it not be because you were vague in what you presented.

MUSIC NOTATION

In chapter 5, I discussed using various forms of music notation, both formal and informal, in the writing process itself. If you've been working this way already, hopefully, you'll have versions close to fair copy for notation. If you haven't produced notation as of yet, you've likely been using audio recordings as de facto "notation."

As you finalize the song, consider making the effort to work up more formal written notation. This serves several purposes:

- First, like a fair copy lyric sheet, notation serves as a "fixer" or definitive version. Preparing a chart requires you to externalize decisions you may have made capriciously and inconsistently (or allowed to stay by default) about phrasing, timing, extra or unbalanced bars and phrases, etc. There's something powerful about creating a chart which must provide a *faithful representation of time* in the song.

- Notation also provides a means of communication with session musicians, demo vocalists, and—depending on the genre—artists.

- Lastly, notation does further document the song from the standpoint of intellectual property protection and copyright, even if it has become more common to register songs using audio recordings.

Industry norms and conventions for different kinds of notation vary across genres and musical communities. In the Nashville studio environment, it's unusual to provide a traditional lead sheet (staff notation of melody, with lyrics and chords). A demo vocalist would typically expect to learn a song from a writer's work demo and an accompanying lyric sheet. In genres such as musical theater or cabaret, a lead sheet would be more commonly expected, or even a notated melody and lyrics with a fully written-out piano accompaniment.

Chord Charts

If you have written without a chart, now is the time to make one! But even if you have prepared one, when finalizing the song, and particularly in preparing for a demo session, the chord chart shifts its purpose from aiding composition to one of communication.

This may require reformatting. For example, my own charts contain additional annotations for aspects like harmonic rhythm. When it's time to turn that chart over to session musicians, I streamline and simplify these elements. Even if you will be the one playing the instrument on the demo and don't think you'll need it, write out the chart as if it will *not* be you playing. That will keep you honest—about things like the actual amount of bars and beats you are spending on chords, for example.

Though I usually won't provide a chord chart until interest is expressed in the song, having a chart readily available for the song is a real advantage. Artists getting ready to record are always very busy. Having ready access to your chart eliminates at least one obstacle, and may encourage the artist or session musicians to give it a run-through. Once you do get a song placed, providing your chart helps to ensure that the eventual cut is closer to the way you envisioned the song. Of course, artists, bands, and producers have their own ideas, tastes, and preferences—and they need to make a song their own. Still, your own chart can communicate unusual musical elements in the "bones" of your song, demonstrating that these aspects are *intended*, are *playable*, and make musical sense. Though the artist, producer, or musicians may still change things, there is less chance that details you care about will get rubbed off in translation, purely by accident.

Lead Sheets

As noted above, formal lead sheets (melody and lyrics, with chord symbols above the staff notation) are not used in all genres or recording environments. Nevertheless, there are significant benefits to having the skills to notate your songs, and to preparing lead sheets as part of finalizing songs, especially in advance of studio demo sessions with other vocalists. For one thing, in preparing the vocal melody on the lead sheet you must make decisions about which melodic figures are aspects of your own individual phrasing, and which are more essential to the song.

A lead sheet can also be an important vehicle for making sure co-writers are really on the same page in terms of detailed decisions around melody, lyric phrasing, and chord choices. Often, getting a clean enough work demo that represents all the decisions made can be quite difficult. If you are relying only on the work demo as your reference point, there is room for many unresolved issues that will only crop up in the studio demo session.

THE STUDIO VOCAL DEMO

It's worth considering distinct stages of the demoing process from a workflow standpoint:

- **Sketches.** Audio fragments and snippets caught during writing sessions may include only portions of the song, multiple attempts or iterations, or multiple co-writers singing slightly different versions of the melody at the same time!

- **Work demo.** A "snapshot" version of the whole song, captured during, or especially at the end of, a particular working session.

- **Reference demo.** The closest thing to a fair copy of the song in terms of a demo: incorporating final decisions for the song, still sung by the writer or one of the writers.

- **Scratch demo.** A demo, often with a writer singing a "scratch" vocal, that is part of the preparation for a demo with a vocalist selected for the song. This might be prepared in advance of the demo session or done as a "scratch" track during the session.

- **Studio vocal demo.** Demo of the song suitable for pitching to publishers or artists. NOTE: This is still one step away from a recording intended for direct release by an artist.

From the standpoint of finalizing the composition stage of the song, this last stage is an audio recording of the song, sung by a vocalist representative of the type of vocalist for whom the song is ultimately intended. For convenience, I call this the *studio vocal demo.* (The term is imprecise: if you have access to a studio for writing, your early sketches, drafts, and incremental versions of work demos might all be "studio" demos. Conversely, an experienced producer working "in the box" might not produce this final demo in an actual studio!)

When it's time to produce the studio vocal demo, additions and adaptations of formats for some materials may prove useful. Some vocalists appreciate having a lyric sheet at the session in a format that accommodates their own markup. A slightly larger font can ease legibility at a distance; a smaller font might keep things on one page. Some vocalists prefer ALL CAPS (though as I said above, I admit to personal bias against this format).

It can also be helpful to provide vocalists a lyric with wider, even double-spaced lines, so they can write in annotations for specific lyrics, such as marking breaths or reminders for tricky melodic passages. (I saw one veteran Nashville session vocalist use a modified "number" notation to indicate melodic tones: e.g., 5 6 1 <u>321</u> 3 for the first line of "Amazing Grace.") Write out full repetitions of chorus sections rather than using placeholders. Even with no lyric differences, singers may want to note alternatives, e.g., for the first versus second chorus.

It is a courtesy to provide a lyric sheet for everyone who will be in the studio booth. Obviously, the designated producer will want their copy. So should the engineer; good engineers know song form, so having the lyric ready at hand will help them set edit points, move to specific sections, etc. It's also a gesture of respect that includes them in considering the overall song and its intent.

Unlike the vocalist's lyric sheet, these need not be double-spaced. Copying all sections out in full is useful, though, for "comping" vocals and other tracks—listening to multiple takes and deciding which to use for particular sections. In this stage, the lyric sheet becomes a handy comping markup sheet. The repeated lyrics provide space to annotate each line performed.

Prepping the Vocalist

Send the vocalist, in advance, a *work demo* of the song: your best rendition of how you want the song to sound, given your own vocal qualities and range.

An experienced demo vocalist will evaluate the song in terms of their range and should be able to provide a preferred key or range of keys. This is especially important if you want backing tracks prepared before the vocal session. Be forewarned: accurately keying a song is a deceptively difficult skill. Sometimes, it's not obvious where high and low points are in melodic contour, and it matters whether the singer needs to belt or just glance off those peaks and valleys. Vocalists also need to gauge the dynamic levels they will need for the song. Getting it wrong can lead to costly mistakes in terms of production schedules, backing tracks, etc.

If you have time for a back-and-forth of materials, it is great to resend the vocalist a practice demo in their preferred key.

A "mock-up" work demo in the proper key and tempo lets the vocalist double-check those parameters and practice to the track. MIDI or DAW tracking is really useful in this case; you can easily shift pitch and tempo separately for virtual instruments. (It's also possible to do this with recorded live instruments; sound quality may be weird if shifts are extreme, but it can serve well enough for the purposes of a practice demo.) You can even have the vocalist send back sketches of high and low spots of the song to check the key.

The Demo Session

For typical pop songs, it's reasonable to expect vocalists to memorize the melody from a work demo before the session, rather than sight-reading from a lead sheet. One value of providing a lead sheet, where possible, as a supplement to your songwriter's scratch vocal demo, is not for the vocalist to sing directly from the lead sheet, but rather as an aid and cross-check for recognizing which specific melodic phrases you want sung as on the demo. (On occasion, experienced demo vocalists have helpfully "fixed" my melody, assuming that those weird, frog-throated modal yodels couldn't *possibly* be what I wanted! Yet sometimes, they were.)

Don't expect the singers to memorize lyrics. That's what the vocalist's lyric sheet is for.

In a typical song session, as opposed to a band chart where parts are written out for each player, provide the session musicians with a work demo and a *chord chart*. It is also helpful to provide a lyric sheet to each player (as to the producer and engineer), and a lead sheet (if you have one) on request.

If you are preparing a demo intending to pitch it to an artist or for a specific genre, share that information with the session vocalist and instrumentalists. The vocalist might need to record over a relatively spare rhythm track, to be filled out later with more instruments and/or production. The singer needs to know—and/or you need to coach them to find—the right energy and dynamic level for the performance, given final production plans for the demo.

If there is a live rhythm section, you will probably want to first lay down a *scratch vocal*—a throwaway track done in the studio, to be replaced later by the "keeper" vocal. The scratch track might be done by the demo vocalist, or by the writer—keeping in mind that this track, unlike a writer's work demo, has to be in the right key, tempo, etc., for the final vocalist.

The vocalist will then lay down final vocals, working with co-writers/producers on details of phrasing, melodic variations, and expression. With adequate preparation, a demo-quality vocal should require not more than a couple hours. Allow time (and budget) for extra work such as overdubs of harmony vocals, or singing alternate lines for alternate mixes.

Aligning with Your Co-Writer(s)

Over time, I have come to appreciate how critical the demo process is in working with co-writers. Even with thorough fair copy lyric sheets and lead sheets, inevitably there are small details that only become apparent during the demo process. You may think you have consensus with your co-writers on these small details, until the time comes to work with the vocalist on lyric issues, phrasing, chord choices, etc.

To minimize such issues at the demo session, there are two strategies, each presenting its own challenges. If all co-writers are present at the demo session, it can morph into a final (or not so final!) revision session for the song. Contention or conflict in decision-making among co-writers can devolve into feuds in the control booth, uncomfortable for all concerned and confusing for the poor vocalist. (I've lived through and made others live through this, and don't recommend it!) Careful preparation and sign-off on fair copy materials before the session is not just for prepping vocalist and players; it nudges co-writers to confront and resolve as many as possible of these lurking decisions.

The other alternative is to designate one co-writer as the producer for the demo session. This makes sense, of course, if one co-writer has access to a recording environment and production experience. The co-writer/session producer should still commit to representing the consensus of the writing team as best they can, and avoid sneaking in unilateral choices during the session that might cause problems later. Thus, advance preparation is just as essential in this scenario.

Alternative Demos

There are often reasons to create multiple demo versions for songs. I remember hearing from veteran songwriter Carl Jackson how, at one time, he routinely cut multiple versions of most songs to pitch to artists in different genres. A given song might have a chance to be cut as a hard-driving bluegrass song (requiring a grassy demo—with banjo!), or as a mainstream country song (requiring a slicker studio version, with drums—and *no* banjo!).

Sometimes, it will be unavoidable to do multiple demos as separate sessions. But from the standpoint of efficiency, it is far better to record in a way that lends the material to as much multipurpose use as possible. For a demo that serves as the definitive finalizing version for the song, plan for future alternate versions and alternate uses, and use the session to create as many of these as possible. If the vocalist has sung alternate lines, or alternate or extra sections, mix down those alternate versions at the same time as the primary version.

It's also a good rule of thumb to run an "instrumental only" mix of every song demo. This can be used in various ways. If you place the song in a synchronization usage, such instrumental "stems" can be used along with the full song. If you later need to recut the demo with a different vocalist, you can use the instrumental mix as a better-quality preparation demo for that new vocalist. For that purpose, you might also run a mix with just instrumentals and backing vocals.

Even in more acoustic genres, it can be amazing to listen back to instrumental tracks, to appreciate the magic that great session players work on a routine basis. I remember listening to instrumental mixes from my first full Nashville demo session— done relatively late in my writing career!—with seasoned A-list Nashville studio musicians. I marveled at the spareness of their playing, and the almost telepathic, unrehearsed interaction between the players.

- In track/topline production, besides instrumentals (that is, fully produced tracks sans topline vocals), it is also useful to pull *a cappella* topline vocals as a separate mix. A kind of "mix and match" flexibility in process has evolved in these environments. Tracks get sent out to multiple top-lining teams, but an a cappella topline might also get reproduced with a different track, even shifting the underlying chord progression.

- If a song lends itself to a well-recorded but stripped-down version with just vocal and guitar or piano, I believe there is always value in having that version on hand. In my version of Songwriter Heaven, that would be all you'd need to pitch a great song. But many genres demand far more elaborate demos. If it's possible, therefore, to pull multiple layered mixes from a studio session, those alternate mixes may prove useful. This is particularly true in recording for film and television synchronization placements, where the demo, per se, is really the final recording, not to be pitched to a different artist but used directly. Songwriters in these markets pull many variations of mixes and stems. There is often no better time to do this work than when the session is loaded and fresh in everyone's ears.

- It is also the case that, to efficiently manage and amortize session costs, songwriters will generally queue up sets of songs to demo in a given session, utilizing the same session musicians and vocalists.

The diagram shown in figure 8.1 summarizes the various workflow steps in finalizing the song.

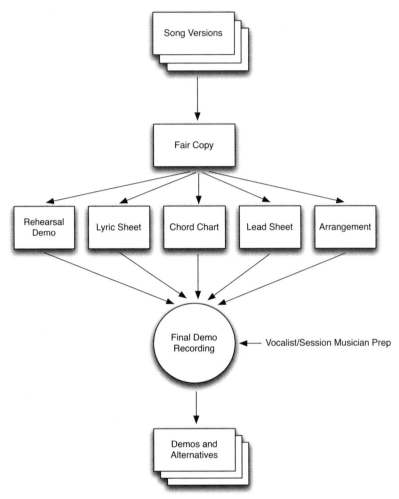

FIG 8.1. Final Steps in the Workflow of Song Development

A Final Word on Finalizing

And finally…

In my first-draft title for this chapter, I used the word "finishing." My final title uses "finalizing." In this chapter, we have been talking about all the stuff that has to happen once the song is *finished*—to make it *final*. It's easy to get impatient with this stage of things. The rush of energy when the major creative work on a song is done, crashing into the attention to minutiae required to dot all the t's and cross all the i's—it's enough to leave you cross-eyed indeed. But it's worth the trouble. Finalizing the song is where you cut all the apron strings that leave aspects of the song dependent on anything in your mind or memory, or floating in conversations and unspoken understandings with your co-writers. It prepares the song to live on its own. Songwriters often feel their songs are their children. When you finalize your song, it's not your baby anymore. It's heading off to college. With a little luck, years from now it may support you in your old age. Or at least, occasionally send a postcard home.

CHAPTER 9

Managing Your Catalog

At the start of our journey, I suggested that, while each song is in a sense its own project, your work as a songwriter is really about managing One Big Project: writing songs and getting them out into the world. To maintain this perspective, at any point in your professional life, you want systems in place—work products and practices—that provide visibility into your *body of work* as a whole, or what is generally called your *catalog*.

Catalog is one of those curious words with a dual meaning. When a songwriter or publisher refers to your catalog, they generally mean the body of songs you have written, completed, and registered for copyright. A publishing deal involving your catalog will typically involve only a subset of this body of work: *active* copyrights—songs released and earning revenue. In another sense, a catalog is a tool—an index, inventory, or database—that provides a view *into* that body of compositions. Think of a Sears Roebuck catalog (or, if you're a songwriter of a certain generation like me, a *Whole Earth Catalog*)—of your songs. In this chapter, we will deal with both of these senses of the word—while also expanding both definitions.

Consider the first sense: your body of work—your *oeuvre*, as it were. In this book, we have explored work products and practices throughout the songwriting life cycle: song seeds, drafts, revisions, co-writing materials, fair copies, demos, etc. Your catalog of published and released work is only the tip of this iceberg of material, which we might call, more broadly, your *creative estate*. (This applies in both a figurative and a quite literal sense. When you depart this mortal coil, anyone dealing with these materials—other than chucking them out for recycling—will be your *estate executor*. Stay with me; we're going to try to make their job easier!) While you're still alive and kicking, effectively managing your publishing and administration catalog depends on your having a handle on all this other material. Think of your creative estate in three tiers:

1. Songs commercially released, either by you or other artists, that are—at least in theory—generating revenue via various licenses, etc.

2. Unpublished songs, registered for copyright, but not yet commercially released.

3. Other creative materials related to your songs, from lists of song seeds, to unfinished drafts sitting in song journals, to song folders on your computer.

A catalog (in the first sense above) might involve material in only the first tier, possibly the second. But managing your entire workflow—including all the other messy stuff and its connection to your published catalog—is vital, both for your creative work itself and for your professional effectiveness.

We will first discuss ways to organize and keep track of your catalog in the first sense: the archive of materials (lyric sheets, notation, audio recordings) that document your songs. Some containers I describe will also help you manage that additional material—your creative estate in the more comprehensive sense. Then we will discuss ways to index and access this material. Lastly, we'll talk about ways to use your catalog as source material for reflection and learning activities, which we'll explore further in the final chapter.

ORGANIZING YOUR CATALOG

As discussed in chapter 5, fundamental *workflow design* choices—e.g., whether you work on paper versus digital, or in bound, consecutive journals versus loose-leaf pages—have pervasive implications and ripple effects. Many of these effects become most visible at the stage of organizing your catalog as a whole.

In my own practice, I made a major transition in the organization of my song catalog. As I described earlier, in my workflow, I prefer to do initial drafts of songs in bound physical journals, transferring material to digital files usually in the later stages of developing songs. So, early on, it seemed natural to me to organize song material by type (lyrics, lead sheets, audio), state of completion (work demos, studio demos), or anticipated next action (songs to final demo, songs to revise). I kept co-written songs in separate folders: dedicated folders for regular co-writers or for one-time or miscellaneous co-writes. In effect, I was using (or attempting to use) these various folders as "action lists" to manage workflow and priorities.

Eventually, I realized that most of my activities were driven by the song itself, and required more centralized access to all the materials for that song at a glance. For example, selecting a list of songs to send to an artist, I would search my lyrics folder as a *de facto* index of my songs. But the lyrics folder wasn't always complete and up to date, and some songs in that folder weren't in a state to be sent out. My system also started breaking down simply because of the number of songs I was dealing with. A system that worked for a few dozen songs just didn't scale to hundreds of songs.

So I did an overhaul, and switched to a catalog system of separate folders for each song. This required me to have some criteria for the cross-over moment when I'd developed a single song sketch or draft enough to warrant its own folder. If you make this transition, be aware that it may take some time—so when you do make a new dedicated song folder, take time *at that time* to gather all the materials for that song from their disparate locations.

In the sections below, I'll provide more details about a system that reflects this fundamental organizational choice. You might find a different approach works better for you. Any protocol you choose will have advantages and disadvantages, will take some discipline to use in a consistent way, and yet will still require workarounds and adjustments. So pick a protocol, stick to it, and refine it over time. Know its limitations, and decide on the workarounds you'll use and the "temptations" you'll try to avoid.

Song Folders

Whether you *generate* creative work on paper or digitally, for a permanent catalog, it is prudent to *retain* material in both physical and digital forms. In fact, any robust system, to some degree, needs to be a blend or hybrid of the two systems, and will require linkage and integration. I maintain what are effectively *song folders* in both physical and digital form. In the physical world, this is a file cabinet with folders alphabetized by song (or tune) title. On the computer, song folders are gathered in a master folder called my—you guessed it!—Song Catalog. The computer and hard-copy song folders, in association, create my full "case history" for the song.

Physical Folders

If you write songs by hand on loose-leaf pages, a one-folder-per-song format is fairly intuitive. My long-time co-writer and "songwriting sister" Lisa Aschmann, who has written thousands of songs with hundreds of co-writers, works primarily with loose-leaf pages on which she hand-writes ideas and drafts. At any given point in a co-writing session, she may have several pages fanned out, with different fragments of material visible. She later gathers all the pages for a given song into a dedicated, labeled folder. When preparing for a subsequent co-write session, she can quickly gather folders for any songs in progress to bring to the session. These folders naturally migrate into an alphabetized archive—in Lisa's case, a shed behind her house, full of four-drawer file cabinets!

Because my main archive is a series of bound journals, my physical song folders serve a slightly different function, and also present some procedural challenges. In the physical song folders, I keep fresh printouts of the *current* fair copy of the lyric and any other notational formats (lead sheet, chord chart) I am maintaining for the song. I also keep printouts of successive versions of the song, and any notes. These are essentially redundant paper backups of what's on the computer, which can also facilitate fast or browsing access. I also keep copies of any loose handwritten material generated at any point in the writing process. This might include printed versions of lyrics that have hand annotations from co-write or critique sessions, or from solo revision work. Since these annotations eventually migrate into fair copy versions, this material is stored mostly for archival purposes and as process history.

The song may initially have evolved over a series of work sessions, documented in the journals. Although I do make safety copies of journal pages, I'll move scans of those pages into the physical song folder only when workflow facilitates it. For example, I may scan and copy non-contiguous session entries for a song being revised in advance of a co-write session. Afterward, I'll archive those pages in the physical folder. But generally, if I need access to those journal entries, I can find them through the journal index described below. (In an ideal archival world, I suppose I might cannibalize one physical scanned copy of my written journals and distribute all the entries into their respective song folders. Anyone want an office admin job?)

Computer Folders

On the computer, each song folder has a common set of subfolders:

- **Lyrics**. I keep an editable version of the current lyric, a PDF version ready to send out, and any alternate versions, such as a public (less contact info) lyric sheet.

- **Charts and Lead Sheets**. If prepared for the song, these might be conventional charts or Nashville Number charts. I'll also keep arrangement materials prepared for demo sessions here.

- **Covers**. If a song has been released commercially, I keep full audio versions of those recordings here.

- **Demos**. Here, I keep all "active" demos of the song, including any viable or current alternate versions.

- **Notes**. Here I put any log materials or written notes about the origin of the song, as well as reflections about discoveries made in the course of writing the song, what the song meant to me, insights gleaned, problems encountered, etc. Sometimes, these are written for demo singers and players in advance of a session, to help them prepare. Sometimes, they are part of the pitch to an artist, providing background on the song that might interest them or make them more likely to engage with the song.

- **Superceded**. In this folder I keep any *older versions* and *revisions* of any of this material: lyrics, notation, demos, etc. This is primarily for archival purposes.

Rarely, there may be a professional reason to dig in to the Superceded folder. For example, after a vocalist has demoed a song, that demo goes into the Demos folder; I relegate my old work demo, with my scratch (often scratchy!) demo, to Superceded land, since it's no longer the active or "live" demo I'd send out. On occasion though, an artist might want to hear my original writer's demo. If I need to re-demo the song with a different vocalist, I may want that demo vocalist to refer back to my original version rather than, or in tandem with, the previous vocalist's version.

But the most important role of the Superceded folder is as my own "process history." It can be very revealing to trace the evolution of a song, especially when I have generated multiple versions over time. For a few songs, such as those on my album *Crazy Faith*, I made and preserved more than a dozen "snapshot revisions."

Journal Index

Though I keep song drafts in consecutive bound journals, I want a way to locate and access material anywhere in that journal repository. To facilitate this, I keep a spreadsheet inventory that lists each journal by number, type of content in the journal (songs, instrumental tunes, teaching notes, etc.), physical format of the journal (I use different formats for different kinds of material, and I also keep experimenting with different sizes and layouts), starting and ending dates of journal entries, number of pages, and archival status (whether the journal has been copied or scanned). With this system in place, I can make a pretty good claim for the date of creation of most of my original work, should it come to that. If the journal has a table of contents, I'll also include the number of items (songs, entries, etc.) in the journal, and keep track of which tables of contents have been transcribed (see below).

Table of Contents Lists

Coordinated with this journal index, I transcribe (or pay to have transcribed!) the *table of contents* for each journal into additional spreadsheet files.

This has proved to be the critical link between my physical and digital archives. Once those contents can be searched, they become much more useful. Often, I remember a working title but not the time frame or context when I worked on it; a simple text search through the transcribed table of contents gets me to the song. Even if I don't remember exactly when I wrote a song, I can search for the song by name, or by co-writer, rather than leafing hopefully through physical journals.

Audio Archives

Handling sketches and drafts in audio formats is similar in principle to handling entries in a journal table of contents. As discussed in chapter 3, chronological information is often essential context when accessing a particular audio sketch later. Sometimes, though, a system-generated name for the file is nothing *but* a date and timestamp. Be careful not to handle the audio in a way that destroys or obscures this information.

If you do rename your audio clips, besides making sure you have not made the date and timestamp impossible or awkward to retrieve, be careful not to try to use the filename itself to convey too much information. Consider portability issues, both for your own maintenance and if you are going to send files to others. Different computer systems have varying restrictions on character sets in names; stick with underscores and hyphens, to be safe.

Also, use caution when your cataloging activity results in transferring audio files to different formats. Various compression formats can significantly degrade audio quality. You may be thinking of the audio clips as "sketches" only. But you never know when an audio source file, even one created very informally and improvisationally, might become a true audio artifact you want to incorporate directly into a mix. At minimum, preserve a copy of the original version somewhere, at the original resolution and quality level.

In order to *not* overload the naming system for audio tracks, I index and inventory audio materials—as with the journal index and transcribed table of contents—in spreadsheet format. Parallel to my journal index, I have an index of the individual media on which collections of audio material are stored. Over my long, storied (or rather, checkered) career, I've recorded song drafts and demos on half-inch home recorder reel-to-reel tape, cassette, microcassette, Portastudio multitrack cassettes, DAT tapes (including mystery tapes that have come unspooled), two-inch studio tape, burned CDs, and varied high- and low-fi digital audio formats; and stored them on oak shelves, desktop computers, laptops, phones, thumb drives, and now—somewhat hesitantly—various formations of the Cloud.

As time allows, I gradually create, in effect, table of contents lists for each of these media collections, as I transfer the materials onto archivable digital formats, amenable to backup storage. I'll discuss some helpful inventorying challenges and strategies further below.

Backups and Safety Copies

In our day of digital copies, amid threats of global warming floods and other disasters, it is prudent to store *safety backups* of all material in at least one other location besides your physical dwelling. If you use bound journals, it is easiest to make a physical copy of the pages—unfortunately a labor-intensive and error-prone task. (Here's where writing boldly in dark black ink, on pages that don't bleed through, and not crowding your margins, helps!) Once you have that copy, you can make an additional safety scan to PDF. Personally, I would then consider storing a copy of both the digital information and the physical safety copy at different premises than your physical journal archive.

Any sort of safety backup protocol presents procedural issues, since songs continue to change over time. But these data storage and security problems aren't really that unique to us as songwriters, so I will leave these larger issues to others more knowledgeable.

SONG CATALOG AS INDEX

Let's assume we have an archive of actual materials for our songs. How shall we maintain an index for that archive? This index is our *catalog* in the second sense: the map of the territory.

I use the word "database" advisedly here. Many songwriters of earlier eras no doubt managed to maintain quite efficient databases on 3x5 cards in oak cabinets. Different kinds of cataloging technologies are best-suited for managing certain kinds of material: databases (for complete songs), spreadsheets (for inventories), and text lists and outliners (for disparate seeds).

Song Catalog Database

For tracking relatively complete songs, I use a relational database system (FileMaker Pro for Mac). Since I set up my system, many new applications have been developed—both specialized tools that run on your own platform, and Web-based tools that store information in centralized repositories.

Whatever tool you select, here are some issues to keep in mind:

- You may be enticed by systems and applications that claim to manage the whole process for you. This can only be accomplished if system designers build in lots of assumptions about how a creative workflow will typically work. Where your workflow might depart from that model, you will hit stress points with the tool.

  For similar reasons, I'd be cautious about outsourcing all your publishing information to a Web-based system. But hey—I'm old-school, and still struggle to get fully "on my Cloud."

- If instead, you opt to build your system from more general-purpose technologies (as I did with my own song database), you face a different trade-off. If you are technology-shy, you may opt for minimal support, and wind up deriving minimal benefits. If you are more tech-savvy, you may get a little too enamored of your system, over-building and over-complicating it with ambitious features and fields you won't be able to support. No tool is magic; you must still build supporting practices around it.

- Expect a certain amount of hand-wringing as you confront all the little details that previously slipped through the cracks. You will come across forgotten songs, open loops, demo projects left dangling, etc. That's inevitable in a creative endeavor that involves moving a multitude of relatively "small-grained" creative projects through many stages of tentative revision, completion, and realization in recorded form. The cataloging *activity* is, by its nature, where the chicken meets the road, and where the rubber comes home to roost (and where you find some rubber chickens too).

- Conceive of the database as a container for *metadata* about the songs, not actual song content. At one point, I tried keeping full lyrics in the database. There turned out to be little value in this, given the ease of text searching in files and folders. And it's a *lot* of trouble to keep aligned with changing and alternate lyric versions.

Seeds, Drafts, Songs

As with physical song folders, you need clear criteria for what material is and isn't handled in this system. It should be more inclusive than the catalog information you share with external entities such as the copyright registry, PROs, publishing and administration companies, labels, etc. In fact, it will be a primary way you coordinate with these entities. But it can't track all your initial inspirations, sketches, and drafts.

At one time, I made the mistake of trying to archive song *seeds* in my database. The result was orphaned material I couldn't access (and will eventually need to clean out). Another one of my bad ideas. (Song seed!)

A lyric seed is basically a scrap of text, perhaps with some stray supporting notes. It doesn't make sense to archive seeds in individual titled files, since it's not much use looking at a list of files with titles like: "Lyric seed . . . Lyric seed . . . Lyric seed (really good!)." A seed is a fragment so small that the best way to name the seed is—the seed! (This becomes particularly obvious when the seed *is* a title.) For similar reasons, it's simply overkill to keep lyric seeds in a database; there just isn't enough to say about each entry. It also dilutes the usefulness of the database as an inventory of relatively complete songs.

My preferred tool for cataloging seeds is not a plain word processor, but an *outlining* tool. For me, moving seeds around, and especially into different bins (representing categories) is an important part of handling them. One disadvantage is that in this format, you put a seed in only one place in the hierarchy. You might have a title seed, which is also one of your seeds about Greek mythology, which is also a seed you know you need to co-write with someone (who also knows about Greek mythology). You could make multiple copies, but that starts to defeat the focusing power of your single, centralized seed catalog. An alternative is to extend the outline with columns, or use a spreadsheet, allowing columns or fields to tag seeds with *multiple* attributes (lyric seed), or to use a free text field for notes that can include tags and search terms.

Similarly, my journals are full of song drafts that include many incomplete fragments. The journal index, linked with transcribed tables of contents, has proved the best way of accessing that information. For me, the transition to a typed lyric or a work demo is a reasonably practical point at which to enter the song in the database.

Inventories of Audio Material

The nature of creative work captured via audio recordings presents some challenges in making useful inventories of these materials. Unless you are skilled at notation, you will capture many musical seeds (melodic, rhythmic, harmonic, sounds, even voice memos of lyric ideas and concepts) as audio recordings, in similar formats and on the same lists as longer sketches, improvisational jams, co-write session recordings, etc. This tends to blur boundaries between true seeds and longer sketches. You might start recording intending to capture only a short seed, and three minutes later have a draft of a song. Thus, in the audio realm it's inherently harder to separate seeds from sketches, and often hard to name audio fragments in a useful way.

These naming problems in cataloging musical seeds are similar, in some respects, to those mentioned above as a reason to avoid putting lyric seeds into a database. Unlike lyric seeds, however, you need to listen to an audio fragment to assess whether it will be useful in a given creative context. It's just not all that helpful to view a list of audio clips with notes like: "Melody seed . . . Chord seed . . . Melody seed (good one!)." This listening takes time. And, in most contexts besides browsing for general inspiration, scrolling through accumulated musical sketches by listening to each in turn is too slow to be practical.

I have learned that by far the *best* time to generate a descriptive label for an audio fragment is *immediately after recording it.* It does take an extra moment, and might require some housekeeping given the format and recording tool used. But you will never have more context. (As Rabbi Hillel says, "If not now, when?")

Another ideal time to review and label audio materials is when you have an *actionable* outcome in mind, but are not under direct time pressure, as you would be during an in-person co-write session. For example, you can work through materials to queue a batch of audio sketches to send "over the wall" to a co-writer in advance of, or even in lieu of, face-to-face co-writing. This is essentially how contemporary producers work when sending beats or fully produced tracks out to one or more toplining teams. (See the discussion of over-the-wall co-writing in chapter 7.)

Another good opportunity to catalog audio seeds is at low-energy times, when you do at least have time and attention to work on a sketch inspired by one of the musical seeds. In effect, you can use audio content transcription as a prelude to an Appointment with Inspiration.

Whether or not you have a project context or an Appointment with Inspiration, listen through audio archives when you can also take the time to work on description and cataloging. This will slightly slow your listening, but now, your listening pass is doing multiple duties. Even if you stop when you find a seed or sketch to work with and don't finish the cataloging work at that time, you're at least chipping away at the workflow management task.

For each entry, list the file name of the audio clip (how you can find it), the date and time created, and the length of the clip. (Usually, all this information is available programmatically.)

Then, annotate the following information in a text notes field:

- What's on the recording. Voice only? Piano plus voice? Guitar only?

- Note if the audio is a sketch for a song in progress: "'Blowing in the Breeze'—Sketch." For a series of sketch takes, note the sequence in which they were recorded. The time stamp should tell you that, but it's good practice to also name them appropriately: Sketch 1, Sketch 2, etc.

- If there are sung lyrics on the recording, list a key phrase, or what you expect the title will be, or a first line.

- Add any other useful descriptors, e.g., for tempo (fast, mid, slow), style or genre ("Irish-y"), mood, section(s) included ("melody for R&B chorus").

Don't take too much time for all this, or you may never go back to it again. The best way to maintain focus is to imagine contexts in which you will be reading through your own descriptions later: using scan-and-match to find a musical idea in a co-write session; or responding to a request from a client, such as a music supervisor or an A&R rep, who may be expressing their preferences in similar loose, vague, or impressionistic descriptions. How can *you now* best communicate to *you then* what that audio seed or sketch sounds like?

Suggested Database Information

Here's a quick rundown of suggested fields for a relatively comprehensive song database system.

- **Song/tune name**. I write a lot of instrumental music as well as songs. I wavered over whether to maintain these in separate catalogs, and eventually opted to keep them together. There are cases where a work begins as instrumental only, then later has lyrics added, either by me or by others. This means that there are irrelevant fields for each type of compositional work. (You can, if it's worth it, create alternate views in the database to support these different types of material.)

- **Status**. This is an indication of how far along in the writing process a given song is. It allows for drafts, works in progress, completed songs needing demos, demoed songs, etc.

- **Version number**. This should reflect the latest version of the song, corresponding to version numbers in the lyric sheets and lead sheets.

- **Demos**. This is one part of the database that requires a one-to-many mapping; although there may be a progressive series of demos of a song, there may also be alternate versions that are "live" at any given time, for different usages. It's worth tracking each of these in the database, with one indicated as primary. One problem is keeping revisions of songs aligned with demos, which often lag behind revision work and reflect earlier versions. I don't think the database is the place to retain the full version history reflected in the physical and digital song folders. However, it is worth including the version number with information about the demo.

- **Co-writer(s), co-publisher(s), and percentages**. Your database should be adequate to store at least the information shown on a typical split sheet. In these days of team collaboration, there can be quite a number of co-writers listed on some songs.

  You will want to retain contact information for all co-writers involved on songs that are being actively worked (as discussed in chapter 7). However, it makes sense to retain publishing information for each co-writer on a per-song basis. If you have long-term relationships with co-writers, their publishing affiliations may shift (as may yours) for different songs, so this information belongs with the song.

- **Registration tracking**. I store the date the song was entered into the database, and the date the song was considered "complete" (complete enough to register for a copyright). At one point, I had dates that tracked the paper trail of mail deliveries to the copyright office; now that is mostly handled digitally. I also track date the database record itself was last modified. I also retain information on the song such as the copyright registration number and date, PRO registration and date, etc.

- **Notes**. This is an important field, which you can use for anything that doesn't fit into the other fields. I generally keep extensive musings on songs in a separate document, as part of the song folder.

  This field can become a magnet for ephemeral information like the status of various pitches, etc. Be attentive to where you might start to make your *song* database do multiple duty as the kind of pitch tracking record-keeping system a publisher or song plugger needs to maintain. Which leads us to . . .

- **Descriptors**. Create whatever fields make sense to you, given the ways you categorize the kinds of songs you write: by genre, theme, gender, "emotional temperature," etc. Unlike "genre" fields in a public music service, your vocabulary doesn't have to conform to anyone else's, since you are the one doing the translation. (I doubt too many other songwriters have all the same set of genre names as me, including genres like "Cosmic," "Non-Sectarian Gospel," "Québécois/Cape Breton," "Trans-Ethnic," etc.) I find that these fields can present opportunities for looking for thematic groupings of songs that might lend themselves to particular collection projects. You might also be working with an external party like a publisher, label, library, etc., that has its own keyword or search term system. You'll still want to maintain "ownership" of your own tags and keywords for your songs.

- **Archival information**. I include information in the database that links the song to archival materials, such as journals. I will include the journal number and entry number for the song, if available. If it was originally written in a loose-leaf format that remains in the archive, I'll indicate this. I also have a checklist of which materials have been prepared for the song: lyric sheet, lead sheet, and chord chart.

- **Musical parameters**. Although this is more laborious to track, I have found it useful to record information about the song that includes attributes such as scale/mode, time signature, tempo range, and song form (perhaps as detailed as listing the specific sectional structure). Note that I haven't listed the *key* of the song; although in practice, you play in a key when you write a song, that doesn't mean the song must always be in that key. You'll pick a key for a demo vocalist and an artist will similarly pick their key. What *is* an attribute of the song itself, however, is the vocal *range*, and that can be quite interesting to catalog. Similarly, although you write a song in a time signature and a rough tempo, each demo and each master recording may subtly adjust that tempo. (In fact, tempo shifts are often one of the factors that leads to trying a different demo to get the right feel for a song.)

This is labor-intensive information to record, if you haven't noted it in the process of writing the song. You might have to listen through the whole song to determine some of these attributes. Depending on how long you've been writing songs and how many you have, you may not be able to devote days or weeks to retroactively entering this information en masse. However, if you are setting up your database early in your career, get in the habit of recording this information routinely when cataloging newly finished songs. There are many potential payoffs to having this information readily on hand. For example, it can help you rapidly narrow down candidates for a specific pitch opportunity. Its most important use, though, may be to aid self-assessment, such as the "gap analysis" of your catalog as a whole that we discuss in chapter 10.

- **Cover recordings**. As noted above, pitch information is highly ephemeral, time-sensitive, and complex (in terms of tracking how many songs were sent, in what sequence, via what media, etc.). As a result, it doesn't really sit that well in your song database.

  On the other hand, cover recordings, along with your own artist's recordings, are—in many ways—the point of this whole great Songwriting Endeavor. These are definitely associated with each song. And, although it would be awfully nice if new cover recordings were daily events, chances are they will be less frequent occurrences. It makes sense, therefore, to include this information with each song.

  I maintain fields for all cover recordings of the song, including the artist, label, album title, and date of release. This field could also include information like synchronization placements.

I also include the specific title under which the song was released, which could vary from the working title in your song materials, perhaps even from your title of record in the copyright registration. In some cases, this might require you to file an amended copyright, or, if you registered the song as an unpublished work, to file an additional registration as a published work listing the alternate title.

You will want to allow for *multiple cover recordings* of your song. Many classic songs have been recorded hundreds of times. So—fingers crossed! (And what better use for a repeating field in a database?)

You will also want a separate list of all your cover recordings, for coordinating with copyright registration, PRO licensing, royalty collection, etc. This overlaps into the music business management part of your practice, and is beyond our scope to cover thoroughly here.

CONNECTING SONGS TO OPPORTUNITIES

We've described a system where song folders archive song *content*, while your catalog tracks *metadata*, information *about* your songs. This includes some legal and contractual information about the song as intellectual property: copyrights, PRO registration, cover recordings and licenses, etc.

A host of other essential information concerns ways to connect songs to opportunities in the world. As we touch on these topics, we reach the boundary of what can effectively be covered thoroughly in this book. Here, however, are a few suggestions about essential ancillary lists to support your catalog management.

Pitch Information

At one time, I tried to maintain detailed information about song pitches in my song database, as a set of "sent to" records for each song. There are advantages to including this information in the database. For example, you can see at a glance how often and to whom a given song was pitched. Eventually, though, I found this organization to be problematic. It is very easy for this information to get out of sync if you (or a publisher or plugger working on your behalf) are doing a lot of active pitching.

I now maintain pitch information outside the database, in ancillary spreadsheets and logs. My main organization for this information is by recipient rather than by song. When you are in a position to pitch material over time to the same artists, it becomes more important to know which songs you sent that artist last, and how long ago, than to know how many and what other people have heard the song. In the "good old days" when you pitched songs for consideration, you could expect definitive responses: "Pass" (not interested), "Maybe," "Put on Hold," "Accepted," etc. It's a different world now: with many more indirect ways of getting songs heard, but also with everyone so busy, you often feel you are dropping songs down a bottomless well where you don't hear even a splash. In contemporary plugging practice, songs are often in circulation to multiple parties.

So I keep a separate spreadsheet for each pitch "client." For a given pitch opportunity, which often involves sending multiple songs, I first do a sweep through my catalog to assemble a list of candidates, factoring in any guidelines I've received about the type of material they're looking for, or gaps still to be filled on a late-stage project. I prioritize, then whittle down the candidates to a short list, and then note information about the final pitch: the date sent; the direct recipient and (as a separate field) targeted artist or placement; which songs, versions, and demo versions were sent; and the sequencing of songs (if applicable). This system has survived various changes of preferred media for delivery (paralleling, to some degree, the changes of archival format mentioned earlier): from cassettes (whoops—dated myself there!) to CDs, MP3 attachments, Dropbox folders, and on into the future when songs will be pitched by direct telepathic transmission. (*Love* this song—I *will* you to!)

List of Artists and Prospects

Do you have standing relationships with artists or other song placement opportunities? When an artist records your material, an ongoing connection is established, which you can nurture by offering "first listens" to new material, and by responding promptly and enthusiastically to requests for material for a new project. If you're working in film and television placements, you will probably cultivate, directly or through a publisher, certain music supervisors open to working with you.

You need to feel out on a case-by-case basis whether a given artist or placement connection enables you to "push" unsolicited material at regular intervals or prefers you to respond to requests, and whether you can send songs individually versus batched, etc. But you can establish regular, *proactive* practices supporting each type of relationship:

- Completion of a song or co-write: Scan your list for artists open to receiving "pushed" material, for whom the song might be a good match.

- Appointments with Opportunity: Just as you keep song seed lists vital by regularly returning to them to develop songs, regularly return to your artist lists and send unprompted pitches to those open to receiving them. If not now, then when? And if not you, then who?

Connection to Publishers, PROs, etc.

As I outline all this detailed catalog housekeeping, you may be thinking: This sounds like the kind of system any publisher needs in-house. You're right, but there are a few important distinctions.

First, a true full-service publisher must maintain this information for *many* writers, not just one. I assume here that you are supporting a *solo* songwriting practice—though a not-insignificant part of that practice may well include information about collaborations with co-writers, you likely won't have the level of administrative and procedural support of a large publisher. Unfortunately, if you generate a lot of songs, you must still try to do an adequate job of managing at least your own material as comprehensively as possible.

You can outsource some of the publishing side of your songwriting business to a publisher, an administration company, or a freelance plugger. But the publisher works with information you provide, so you can't really outsource the basic housekeeping. If you don't take care of it, you will have trouble handling even your handoffs to a publisher or administrator. I've learned, painfully over the years, that I don't derive the full benefit of these other relationships if my own house is not in order. I know, it doesn't seem fair!

Furthermore, what you require isn't merely a *subset* of the kind of system a full (multi-songwriter) publishing house maintains; you need to manage the whole flow of creative content leading to the completed song and demo that will be ultimately tracked by your various business partners. This material includes not just earlier drafts and work materials of finished and published songs, but many songs, completed and not, that won't get handled by outside agents of any sort for the foreseeable future. And, as we have seen, it includes the full range of other work products, from seeds to drafts, to pre-writing, to source material. But if you don't do a good job of managing all this ancillary and preparatory material, chances are, you will be a bit disorganized in your eventual interactions with these other business associates.

The diagram shown in figure 9.1 provides a summary of the workflow involving your song catalog.

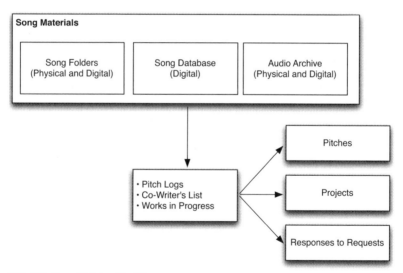

FIG. 9.1. Song Catalog Workflow

WORKING WITH ASSISTANTS

There are some seeming "clerical" tasks that are part of the work of songwriting that you can't easily hand off or delegate. Even if you can, doing so may rob you of some creative benefits of working iteratively with the materials, as we discussed in chapter 4.

But some tasks you *can* hand off, and in the realm of catalog management, we encounter more of those possibilities. You can expect a fair amount of somewhat tedious administrative work when initially entering material into the cataloging system. Typing table of contents lists from bound journals onto spreadsheet files is another easily delegated task. This may therefore be a good point to enlist administrative help, if you can afford it. Once you're working with your catalog, the very lack of context can provide a helpful shakedown; having another pair of eyes (trying to!) make sense of your informal system will be a stress test of what you actually do and don't have documented.

Even if you don't yet have enough material, or prospective revenue, or money to hire an assistant, approach your workflow management *as if* you will turn to an assistant at some point. Yes, that assistant may still be *you*—six months from now, when you have no clear memory of what is foregrounded right now in your attention. Working with, or preparing to work with, an assistant is also good staging for handing material off to external stakeholders.

Your song catalog is the physical and digital embodiment of your songwriting practice and legacy. It's likely the most valuable (non-living) thing in your house. And, by the time you have built the catalog (index) *to* your catalog (your songs), it may well feel like a living thing in its own right. If you have tended to your craft, your catalog will outlast you. Build it to last.

CHAPTER 10

Advancing Your Craft: Reflective Practices

In this book, we've explored a variety of good housekeeping practices for songwriters. We have avoided direct discussions of songwriting craft that are dealt with in many other sources. And, although better catalog management practices, such as those described in chapter 9, certainly position you to respond more effectively to professional opportunities, we have stopped short of describing detailed music business strategies, either for artists or for those writing songs for others. Our focus has been helping you better manage the creative workflow of songwriting. A summary picture of all the workflow work products and activities described in the previous chapters is provided at the end of this chapter.

Undeniably, all this housekeeping is a lot of work! The good news is that workflow management tools and practices provide a number of additional benefits. They also provide a rich base of information and tools to help you:

- Manage the inherent uncertainties of the songwriting profession.

- Reflect on your current practice in ways that can help you advance your craft and take your songwriting in new directions.

SURFING THE CHAOS

As described at the start of this book, one crazy-making aspect of songwriting is how little control you ultimately have over the process. At the front end, inspirations come to you; you can't really decide to have them. At the back end, though you plug doggedly away, the quality of your song is just one of many factors determining whether it gets cut by an artist, or whether your own release becomes a viral hit. To keep working on your craft, you must keep believing the quality of your songs matters. Yet you can't base your sense of self-worth on the world's *directly* recognizing that quality, in any singular instance or on any particular timeframe. Man, it's a tough business. As someone said of a songwriter's life in Nashville, it requires the soul of a poet and the skin of a rhinoceros.

Measuring and Motivation

Though you can't measure success in songwriting like cords of wood chopped, it's at least worth measuring what you *can*, celebrating what successes you achieve, and keeping an eye out for problems you might want to address. Rather than leaving you completely at the mercy of the muse, housekeeping practices provide ways for you to measure certain aspects of your creative work, to stay motivated, and, if necessary, to improve or change your practice.

Your Songwriter's Log

In chapter 6, we discussed the practice of maintaining a song log to document the process of writing and revising a particular song. There is also some value in maintaining a log of your overall progress as a songwriter: your Songwriter's Log.

When I *finish* a song journal and before starting another, I review my productivity in the completed journal. I look at the start and end dates to see how long I spent filling that journal, in relation to the number of songs in the journal. That gives me a rough sense of my pace of writing for that period. Over time, I'll notice fluctuations based on other activities: do I write fewer songs on tour, or during a teaching semester? This kind of review helps us stand back and see our songwriting practice as a whole—as a mighty flowing river—instead of grabbing madly for that fish of a song as it wriggles out of our hands.

Having designated seed pages in my journal back pages provides another useful metric: a rough proportion of seeds to drafted or completed songs. Of course, these numbers *shouldn't* match! I hold to the *abundance principle*: ten seeds for every draft, ten drafts for every finished song, ten songs for every demo, etc. But if, in a given period, you find you have caught many more seeds than you have drafted songs, that might indicate you need more Appointments with Inspiration. If you have very few seeds not turned into drafts and relatively few completed songs, you might need to give yourself permission to collect more ideas and inspirations without the compulsion to develop them all. You can also track simple metrics like how many co-write sessions you scheduled, pitches you made to artists, etc. *Anything under your direct control is worth measuring.*

Listening Log and Journal

You can maintain a songwriter's "captain's log" for more than just your own creative output. A *listening journal* has entries for songs, albums, concerts, and artists you have experienced and been inspired by (or perhaps actively disliked!). The log is, if you will, *diary entries*; you can enrich it with reviews, reflections, observations, and debriefs. This can feed back into your own creative work in a variety of ways: via adaptation projects, where you work from particular songs to create your own work in response; or sharing listening logs with co-writers or colleagues in a local songwriting circle.

REFLECTION AND LEARNING

To advance our songwriting, we want to do better what we already do, and also explore new ways to write. Both goals require spending time noticing and reflecting on our current practice. You can accelerate your growth as a songwriter by integrating these reflection activities directly into your practice and workflow. This requires more *qualitative* review—less about metrics, more "rich descriptions" of what you did, what worked, and what didn't.

Debriefs

Probably the easiest reflective practice to adopt is *debriefing* your creative work. (It's a kinder term than "post mortem," which always sounds like something died.) Debriefing generally requires allowing for a period of reflecting on the process, *after* the creative work is done. It's relatively easy to manage because it happens after the flow of the creative work. But it's best done as soon afterward as possible, ideally, directly after the creative work; otherwise, you will quickly forget some of the more fleeting moments of discovery, or of trouble. Debriefing also provides a place to record contextual information that is at the forefront of your mind in the midst of the creative work, yet may be hard to retrieve coming back to the material later.

Here are questions for reflection, useful for any song:

- Did I set out to do something different with this song than I have done before?

- Whether or not I set out to do something different (an explicit at-the-outset challenge), did I accomplish something different in this song?

  Songwriting is not about practicing your chops and executing the same performance consistently, but finding *novel* creative material. To further advance in your songwriting, you need to also seek out novelty in the ways you write songs (meta-novelty, to get nerdy!). A primary goal of my first book, *Songwriting Strategies*, was to provide songwriters a roadmap for experimenting in different ways with their songwriting process. These self-challenges, or challenges discovered and pursued in the midst of writing, will not always be evident later just from the song itself. It's really helpful to document them while they're fresh.

- Did I get stuck writing this song? If so, *where in the process* did I get stuck? (A more helpful starting point than *why*, it is a bit more objective and requires less speculation about causes.)

Debriefing is an important practice to develop in your solo writing, but it is especially valuable for mastering the more complex and nuanced interactions of co-writing. If you are lucky enough to work with a co-writer who is game to debrief with you, try to schedule some debriefing/reflection time at the end of the session. But even if you must debrief on your own, it's well worth the effort. Expect, though, to encounter some internal resistance to the practice. I joke with my students that debriefing is easy, except in two circumstances: when things have gone really well (because you don't want to jinx your success), and when things have gone badly (because you don't want to have to think about it!). But these are, of course, the very situations we can learn the most from. Your goal should be to leave every writing session—solo or co-write—a better songwriter (and co-writer) than when you started.

Left Page/Right Page

Debriefing happens after the event. But capturing reflections on process is much like catching song seeds: the longer you wait to write them down, the less chance you have of actually remembering the insights. To capture reflections during a songwriting session, any delay affects the level of detail and veracity. At the same time, stepping outside the flow of any foreground task to reflect is inherently disruptive. This is true of the immersive quality of creative work, and especially of collaborative work.

I developed the *Left Page/Right Page* journal format working with Lisa Aschmann. We enjoyed not only the fruits of co-writing but the activity itself so much that we would often step back in the midst of a co-write to debrief a specific creative decision we had just worked through. Over time, I started scribing some of these observations, and eventually found a simple way to negotiate the rhythms of these alternations between immersive creative work and points of reflection. I use the left page of my open journal to record direct creative work (lyrics, sketches, rhyme search lists, occasionally solfege-syllable melody or Nashville chords); I switch over to the page on the right for reflective notes.

This format works particularly well in co-writing, where it minimizes the disruption of shifting between modes of work. Over time, I have adopted it for solo writing as well. At any point, I can choose to either interleave material or use a side-by-side or parallel presentation. I might also use the right-hand page for pre-writing materials, rapid-fire sketches, or material in other facets, such as chord progressions or melodic indications.

You can also use a "hop-over" to the right-hand page strategically, to help manage the flow and rhythm of a writing session— for example, if you hit a lull in your energy, but don't want to disengage completely. In co-writing, you can slow your pace to accommodate your co-writer's working rhythm by using the time to note observations in your right-page "process log."

And sometimes, at moments when you are genuinely stuck as to how to proceed with the song, a move to the right-hand page can provide a needed respite, almost like stepping out of the room for a walk around the block. Material from the right-hand page also may flow back onto the left-hand page. On many occasions, I get an unexpected "gift" from the right-hand page, such as a chance phrase that turns out to be exactly the right image to use in that third verse I haven't begun to write yet.

USING YOUR CATALOG FOR REFLECTION AND SELF-ASSESSMENT

So far, we've discussed ways of using metrics of progress, retrospective debriefing of creative work, and interleaved creative and reflective annotations in the course of active writing and co-writing. Your song catalog also offers possibilities for learning about yourself as a songwriter, at a far more expansive level. You can use your catalog as a whole for self-assessment, and from there create specific challenges to advance your craft and broaden your range and scope as a songwriter.

Looking at the Songs You've Written

It is a surprisingly powerful exercise simply to do a thorough inventory of *all the songs you've written* (and completed) to date. This is a major step in developing a fuller sense of yourself as a songwriter. It will inevitably be a mix of good and bad news. You may be surprised at how many songs, or how few, you've written. You will stumble across forgotten songs you now remember you liked, or be crestfallen to discover fewer real keepers than you'd imagined you had. The process also becomes a personal and autobiographical as well as a creative review. Most of us begin writing songs early enough in life that our creative efforts are infused with—and fused with—our personal trials and travails (no doubt confusing enough to begin with!). Don't be surprised if the process stirs up strong emotions and memories.

Traps and Gaps

You can use your song catalog (the tool, not the archive) to consider almost any aspect of your songwriting tracked in the catalog and assess the "coverage" your current inventory of songs represents. You can look for two kinds of patterns:

- **Traps: "Almost Always," favors**. These are your go-to habits: musical, lyrical, and thematic tendencies that show up in most of your songs—things you almost always do as a writer.

  The hard question: do you use these structures even when they don't really serve the needs of the song?

- **Gaps: "Almost Never," avoids**. These are song elements you almost never use, that are out of your comfort zone. Your emphasis should be not on what you don't do because you *can't*, due to technical limitations ("I don't write songs with advanced harmonic changes because I only know three chords . . . "), but rather on things you *could do, but don't*.

You can apply this "traps and gaps" style of self-assessment to any aspect of your writing that you have thoroughly inventoried in your catalog. This can provide some extra incentive to complete certain passes through your song database. For example, you might make one pass noting the time signature and tempo range of every song in the database. You then discover that 90 percent of your songs are in 4/4 time and were written (and demoed) at 120 beats per minute: a trap (though admittedly, one shared by myriad writers!). You might also discover some gaps, e.g., you have rarely written in 3/4 time, or never in 6/8 time, or you have almost no songs faster than 130 beats per minute, or slower than

90 beats per minute. (Yes, you could artificially change the tempo of a song already written, but many aspects of lyric placement, chord movement, etc. might simply not work.) You can do similar traps-and-gaps analysis on other musical parameters such as your preferred and avoided tonalities and modal colors, the vocal ranges of your melodies, etc.

As you build this profile, you can then start creating self-challenge assignments of two kinds: challenges of *avoidance*, where you take away your go-to techniques and forms and force yourself to try something new; or challenges of *performance*, where you give yourself a particular new device, technique, or form to use. You can play these off in any variety of ways: "toe in the water" incremental challenges, or fiendish ninja "do everything different all at once" crazy challenges.

A NOTE ON SIGNATURE VS. LIMITATION

It's always fair to say you *favor* a certain type of song because "that's what you do," or that you avoid certain kinds of songs because you genuinely don't like them and don't want to write them! The problem is knowing which choices of range and scope represent *authentic choices*—who you really are, and want to be, as a songwriter and creative artist—and which may be expressive of fears, doubts, and self-limitations. Attributing a gap to simple lack of technique or knowledge does not really resolve this question: after all, to some extent at least, you also choose what you decide to *learn* to do, and what you accept that you can't do.

As a writer myself, and as a teacher and coach to songwriters, my attitude is: you only get the information you need to answer these questions by first *trying* what feels beyond your range.

RESOURCES

Throughout this book, we have explored different "containers" to help manage the workflow of your songwriting. These containers serve to control the flow of creative materials: seed and source material, song drafts and versions, etc. Material "flows" through these containers, in the sense that it is unique material that gets "used up" in a given song.

In addition to your original creative material, you will make use in the writing process of some resources that provide constant or canonic content as reference material or tools. Songwriters need to love language, and music, and all the mysterious ways they interweave. So, besides your seed lists of cool phrases and individual words caught on the fly, your songwriter's workbench should include some standard reference materials and resources, similar to those any sort of writer wants on hand.

Lyrical Resources

- **Dictionary.** You can use this basic resource to clarify precise word meanings when sketching, trying alternate versions of lines, or working a lyric seed idea into a clarified concept or narrative frame for a song. Dictionaries also show word origins, and can lead you to sources of metaphors and idiomatic phrases. They also provide syllabic stress patterns for multi-syllable words, critical for checking word-setting and prosody.

- **Thesaurus.** (What's another word for thesaurus?) A thesaurus provides synonyms (and antonyms) for words. Sometimes neglected as a resource for songwriters, as compared to the rhyming dictionary, the thesaurus is a critical resource during sketching and revision. When trying to get from a pretty good line to a killer line, as Mark Twain famously said: "The difference between the almost-right word and the right word is the difference between a lightning-bug and lightning."

  But this doesn't capture the full power of this resource for songwriters in particular. In quintessentially non-linear fashion, we don't always start from a clear concept of what we mean and want to say, then go looking for not just the almost-right but the right word. Rather, we work iteratively between sound and sense, and may shift our intended meaning and emotional shadings of the song in response to subtly varying connotations and nuances of synonyms. Working with a thesaurus can shape not just the details, but the whole emotional focus and direction of the song.

- **Rhyming dictionary.** This is the acknowledged perennial tool of songwriters. There's no doubt that finding rhyme possibilities is one area where there is no particular honor in counting on only rhymes we can retrieve through our limited vocabularies (combined with our typical impatience at moments in songwriting where we need the rhyme).

Whether you use physical print versions of these resources, digital versions, or both is a procedural question that will no doubt change over time for you. While digital versions of these resources will continue to evolve in sophistication, there are advantages to having physical books at hand—not unlike the comparative benefits of drafting songs by hand and on paper, rather than by typing into a computer file. The act of riffling through the dictionary, and visual collisions of what you scan peripherally on the pages, provide opportunities for serendipitous "stumblings over" of material that may be important in your creative work.

Besides these standard resources, you may find it useful to assemble all sorts of additional reference resources to use either for "seed dives" during dry spells, or during sketching and revision:

- Books of idioms and idiomatic phrases, both old and new. One of my prized possessions is a three-volume edition of H.L. Mencken's magisterial *The American Language*, which includes turns of phrase from many earlier (pre-1920s) American regional dialects.

- Collections of proverbs, quotations, riddles, slang expressions, etc. (This might even include the dreaded Urban Dictionary—peruse at your own risk!)

- Links to archives of old newspapers and other historical source material. In his memoir *Chronicles*, Bob Dylan describes spending many hours in the New York Public Library, reading through old newspaper sources. Today, vast archives of such material are available on the Web.

Musical Resources

Besides language-oriented resources, similar sorts of collections of musical materials are also worth keeping on hand. Here are useful resources for rhythm, melody, and chords/harmony:

- Jon Damian's *The Chord Factory* (Berklee Press, 2007)
- Mick Goodrick and Mitch Haupers' *Factorial Rhythm for All Instruments* (Mr. Goodchord, 2005)
- Nicolas Slonimsky's *Thesaurus of Scales and Melodic Patterns* (Literary Licensing LLC, 2012)

Besides these kinds of resources, any technology that offers libraries of sounds, rhythms, samples, loops, grooves, etc. can be used as a starting point for creative work. You could consider these "seeds" in terms of process and the way you work with them, but they have essentially been compiled for you. You need never lack for source material with these resources, be they well-thumbed old-school books or digital data spaces. However, they will always only complement, never replace, seed catching: that essential songwriter's work of keeping your ear to the ground and to the wind, listening for the magical turns of phrase and accidental collisions that you will find compiled in no phrase book or compendium except the big, wide world from which we draw our strongest songs.

Prompts

Prompts are renewable starting points for inspirations. These are worth cataloguing in their own list. You might turn to a prompt to get yourself writing on a morning when you want to write, but lack energy even to riffle through your list of *sui generis* seeds. You can also use prompts as icebreakers for co-writing sessions. In my collaboration classes, I have co-writers pair off as storytellers and scribes, using prompts in the form of questions with ellipses:

- "The first time I ever . . . "
- "The last time I ever . . . "
- "The only time I ever . . . "

These are intended to elicit memories of pivotal personal moments, likely to resonate (at least in retrospect) with some song-worthy emotional intensity.

Many creative writing exercises are given in the form of prompts. Writing teachers prize them—you can give a prompt to a classroom of writers, get a classroom's worth of new and different songs in response, and then use that same prompt again the next semester!

A number of songwriting-oriented books are less concerned with technical discussions of craft, and instead are essentially collections of prompts and creative starting points for songs. Two examples are Lisa Aschmann's *1000 Songwriting Ideas* (Hal Leonard, 2008) and Sheila Davis' *The Songwriters Idea Book* (Writer's Digest Books, 1992).

Over time, besides compiling favorite prompts from other sources, you will also want to build your own library of prompts. Some of these may start as your seeds. Most song seeds are ideas for songs you use once, and then have effectively *used up*. However, as you sort and sift, you may come across seeds that serve more as prompts—individual, personal, "reusable" starting points for new songs. Each will demand a particular kind of creative energy and intensity, and will be useful in different contexts.

One prompt I developed, that I use frequently myself and teach as an exercise to other songwriters, is my "Jackson Pollock" exercise: throw your hand down at random on the guitar or piano, discover a new chord shape, and use that as the seed for a new song. In my own practice, I've used that and similar self-challenge exercises to spark countless writing sessions.

WORKING WITH MULTIPLE SEEDS

By and large, songwriting tends to be fine-grained creative work. When using song seeds as starting points for songs, a good working assumption is "one seed/one song." This helps ensure focus and unity in songwriting, although techniques like scan-and-match do allow us to make judicious use of other seeds and seed lists in later stages of developing songs, and in co-writing.

Some more exploratory and experimental techniques and exercises are made possible by having *lists* of seeds as a starting point. Many of these techniques subvert the one seed/one song rule of thumb, building on the non-linear, indeterminate, random, and serendipitous nature of song seed lists. They may lead to very different kinds of songs. At the very least, they help to create and sustain motivation for more disciplined workflow practices around seed lists. Managing seed lists *is* a lot of work. I find, when I ask myself to do some housekeeping chores, that it's good to build in some rewards for good behavior—and to have some fun!

Songwriters are also most often working at the level of the individual song. If you are a performing songwriter, or involved in a musical theater project, albums or shows do provide natural venues for clustering songs into larger sets. However, these are often long-term, major projects. It can also be useful, and energizing, to have other ways of clustering seeds and songs into larger groupings.

Seed Collisions

Because song seeds wind up in lists in arbitrary juxtapositions, in general there is no reason any two seeds from a given list should fit together in the same song. You can use this very property to create a challenge exercise in out-of-the-box, lateral thinking—sort of a songwriter's version of aleatoric or chance composition. (We could call this exercise: "If John Cage Were a Songwriter, Would His Big Hit Be 4'33" Long?") Simply select two unrelated seeds from a list—as much at random as you dare—and try working them up into a single song. You can work with seeds of the same type, such as two lyric seeds, or seeds of different types, such as a lyric and a melodic seed, or a lyric seed and a chord progression. For the greatest challenge, try interweaving seed material into the same section—that is, set *that* lyric to *that* melody.

These techniques allow you to explore a range of possible effects—between agreement and clash, prosody and counterpoint or irony—in elements of the song. Some mismatches will be comical, some may be downright creepy, and sometimes they simply won't work. Every now and then, though, they will be completely magical.

Song Seed Collages

From one seed/one song to seed collisions, we can progress to working with "bundles" of seeds simultaneously. In this technique, we seek to combine multiple seeds that share a common form or theme into a *single song*. I call this a collage because (1) many seeds are used in one song, and (2) most material in the song for that facet (e.g., most of the lyrics or melody) consists of seeds. A seed collage often involves a concept or topic that lends itself to a *list song*—a litany of similar kinds of things. The seeds may come from a single source, or you might find the common thread by reviewing your collected seeds during consolidation of your lists.

Song Suites and Song Cycles

Besides techniques for using multiple seeds in one song, we can also gather seed "packets" that lend themselves to a related *collection* of songs. If the collection is fairly open-ended, we can refer to these as song *suites*; with a defined sequence or order, they can also be termed *song cycles*.

As you work through your seed lists, you might find seeds that lend themselves to these approaches: not just song seeds but "song cycle" seeds. (To push the seeds metaphor a bit: think of them as seeds for new hybrids that yield not just a new plant, but a new crop!) The idea for a song cycle might come very directly from a seed (a big one!) you jot down, with one or two examples of individual songs that could be part of the cycle. But often, a song series concept arises through the work of reviewing your seed lists as you sort, sift, categorize, and rearrange seeds. At the time that you collected these individual seeds, you didn't necessarily conceive of them as part of a series. The "series-ness" of the seed-tuation (sorry!) only becomes visible as you look over your seeds in the aggregate.

Make a note of the project idea, and start a container where you begin to collect materials, starting with the seeds that sparked the series idea. If and when you decide to work further on this series, you can begin by making a more purposeful *sweep* through Seeds Central to collect other candidate seeds. The series concept now serves as a thematic focus—a lens through which you review your seeds and scan-and-match. You may have already gathered more potential seeds for the project than you would have expected. If you already have a catalog of finished songs, you may also have completed songs relevant to the cycle.

As you sift through already captured seeds, new seed ideas are likely to occur to you, often in rapid succession—a cascade of ideas, a kind of "seed-storming." Moment for moment, such episodes of lateral creative work are some of the most productive time you can spend. You are working at an accustomed pace for writing lines for songs, but each idea is for a *new song*.

Having searched through your current seed lists, you will also now be on the hunt for new seed material. Your songwriter's mind will be primed to notice and capture new seeds relevant to the project.

While the series concept is primarily inspiration for your own writing, it also becomes a kind of searchlight for seeking out related source material, including other people's songs. Such projects thus also provide vital links between the in-breath of inspiration from others' work, and the out-breath of your own original expression.

Song collisions, collages, suites, and cycles allow you to work at larger structural levels than one seed/one song threads. Even with no initial external project focus, these can provide sustained threads of inspiration for songwriting work, creating a concept arc that stretches over a number of different writing sessions. That said, there are many possible strategies for releasing multi-song projects, including albums (in whatever distribution form they might take), and performance settings such as cabaret nights or theatrical work.

You can also parcel out songs from a series or cycle for different projects over time. As the industry moves more fully into digital distribution, there will also be increasing opportunities for "multi-releases": repurposing songs into different virtual albums, playlists, etc., according to overlapping thematic groupings. A love song to your dog might wind up in a song cycle about dogs and a cycle of love songs.

Suites and cycles can also include both solo and collaborative work. A prompt shared with a group of writers can generate a suite of songs with a common theme, to be presented as a collective, collaborative work.

YOUR SONGWRITER LIFE LISTS

Beyond general resources, prompts, and multi-seed projects, you can also cull material from your own creative work over time, or select material from external sources, in ways highly individual to you as a songwriter. I call these your *Songwriter Life Lists*. Though they may be simple lists in format, they can play a significant role in your creative work and in advancing your craft. They also require some supporting practices to sustain that role effectively.

Different sorts of lists serve different purposes, each with a particular connection to your songwriting practice:

- A *checklist* is a planning tool, familiar to those in the organizational management field: a sequenced, structured list of reminders for steps you know you need to follow for any given process. You can maintain a checklist of things to remember at the start of any gig (check mic cables, learn the sound guy's name, brush your teeth) or at the start of a co-write session (ask your co-writer if they're comfortable, offer a cup of coffee, turn off your cellphone). In this sense, your checklists can collectively serve as a sort of *instruction manual* to yourself for all the ways you want to consistently manage your workflow.

- A *brainstorming* list is a different tool: not a pre-existing list, but one you generate in the course of creative work. In workflow terms, a brainstorming list is a *pre-writing* work product that aids you in writing the song.

    When I want to encourage myself to work in a brainstorming or editorializing-free zone, I use making a list as a self-challenge device. To use list-making for generative purposes, part of the art is giving yourself the right target number of items for your list—the number matters![4] In many creative tasks, you can easily think of one alternative; pushing yourself to find an *alternative* alternative, that third possibility, requires coming at the problem a different way. (I'm convinced this is part of why *bridges* in songs— usually the *third* distinct musical section—are often where we find an essential deepening of the theme or counter-view onto the situation.)

- A third type of list, the *cumulative list*, is perhaps the one most salient in the big-picture goal of managing the creative workflow of songwriting. The lifespan of such a list is not confined to a particular generative context for a particular song; it accumulates as you add to it over the course of your ongoing creative work. The seed lists we have worked with throughout this book are cumulative lists of this kind. The list is a call to action, or rather a call to possibility. Every seed on the list is a potential starting point for a song.

---

4. My most important number is *three*. My wife and I have a standing joke: as soon as I say, "There are a couple of things to remember about that," she knows my next words will invariably be, "Actually, there are *three* things to remember…"

Your songwriter life lists can serve different purposes, related to each list type above. Like seed lists, they accumulate over time, but it's the list taken as a whole that provides the creative and learning benefit. Sometimes that outcome is serious learning, and sometimes it's just—well, fun!

Here are a few examples of songwriter life lists, drawn both from other writers' work and from your own.

Songs I Wish I'd Written

All listeners and lovers of songs fall in love with particular songs at particular moments in their lives. But when a songwriter falls in love with a song *as a songwriter* and not only as a listener, it is often a sign that there is some secret in that song they are meant to uncover—a next songwriting lesson they are meant to learn. Your wiser Songwriter Mind is sending you a message: study this song. Delve into it. Figure out why it grabs you so hard. Find that hidden vein of gold to mine for your own song.

Out of sources encountered, or music from your listening log, you can steadily assemble a life list you call "Songs I Wish I'd Written." My Songs I Wish I'd Written list would include James Taylor's "Something in the Way She Moves," Peter Gabriel's "Solsbury Hill," and Lennon and McCartney's "In My Life," among many others. Chronology is not essential for this list. However, if you maintain your list in the order your song love affairs occur, the very sequence of the list becomes a kind of portrait of your shifting musical tastes and loves, and an opportunity for later reflection.

To maintain this list, you need *two* supporting practices: adding songs to the list and having some way of *working actively* with the songs you put on the list (rather than just periodically taking it out, reading it over, and getting depressed because you are not James Taylor or Peter Gabriel).

Adding songs to a life list should not be a casual or frequent event; this list should not have one hundred songs on it. These are not just songs you admire, but songs you know have something *specific* to teach you, that embody or encapsulate something of the writer you aspire to be. A good prompt for a first entry in your

Songs I Wish I'd Written list might be: What's the first song you fell in love with so much that you had to learn to play it? (For me, that song was James Taylor's "Something in the Way She Moves." I marched into McCabe's Guitar Shop in Santa Monica, took one guitar lesson to learn it, then went on my merry way.)

Once you have this list, you can make a practice of yet another kind of appointment: an Appointment with Greatness—that is, to study a great and timeless song. An ideal time for this work is during periods when you are feeling less inspired to write via your ordinary approaches, more receptive than active. Studying a beloved song can flow back into new creative work, by using aspects of the song studied as a model or template, or otherwise adapting lessons learned from its study to new creative work. I call this cycle of honoring, studying, and adapting great work *stealing fire*. You can do such work whenever moved to, but by establishing a life list of Songs I Wish I'd Written, you make stealing fire a regular part of your songwriter's practice.

You can also maintain more granular lists, e.g., of individual lyric lines you wish you'd written. I'd die happy to have written this line, from Jackson Browne's "These Days": "These days I sit on cornerstones/And count the time in quarter-tones to ten." Similarly, you can "scrapbook" favorite musical moments, even particular chord progressions. I still delight at the changes in the chorus of "Heavenly Pop Hit" by New Zealand band the Chills.

Not exactly a life list but a true artifact, a beautiful tradition of many songwriters, singers, and musicians, is to maintain a handwritten journal of the *lyrics* for songs you love and learn to sing. Coming of musical age in the eclectic traditional music scene in California in the 1970s, I can remember seeing my first such lyric commonplace book—although with its decoration and calligraphy, it might have been better characterized as an artist's book—of the Delta Sisters, Frannie Leopold and Jeanie McLerie. Here is one of Frannie's later songbooks.

FIG. 10.1. One of Frannie Leopold's Songbooks

Co-Writer Bucket List

A good way to build energy and professional focus is to keep an aspirational wish list of co-writers you'd love to work with. To serve as a life list, this should be a true bucket list of "blue sky" co-writing partners. Each name on the list should have a "I could die happy if . . . " feeling for you. I recall a songwriting master class with songwriter Janis Ian where she said that the most precious aspect of fame and success to her was *access*: the chance to meet and collaborate with her own musical heroes and heroines.

At one time, I would have said that aspiring to co-write with deceased songwriters was probably an outside shot. However, there have been a surprising number of "posthumous co-writing" projects, and I expect this trend will continue. The fact that this is even possible reflects the long-term value of creative workflow management practices. These kinds of projects generally require curated or "gated" invitations, precisely because the source material is, in some cases, so fragmentary as to be difficult to protect on its own via copyright registration.

Songwriters such as Woody Guthrie have left behind troves of unpublished work and unfinished fragments. Woody's daughter, Nora Guthrie, deftly managed his legacy as president of the Woody Guthrie Foundation, inviting contemporary songwriters to, in effect, collaborate posthumously with Guthrie, which resulted in creative projects such as the *Mermaid Avenue* sessions (Billy Bragg and Wilco, *Mermaid Avenue*, 1998, Elektra Records; *Mermaid Avenue Volume II*, Elektra Records, 2000; *Mermaid Avenue, The Complete Sessions*, Nonesuch, 2012). Similar posthumous collaborations have been done with artists such as Hank Williams (*The Lost Notebooks of Hank Williams*, Egyptian Records/CMF Records/Columbia Records, 2011). Recently, Bob Dylan donated much of his unpublished archive of materials to the University of Tulsa, and some of his unfinished lyric sketches were adapted into full songs by contemporary artists, working with producer T Bone Burnett (The New Basement Tapes, *Lost on the River*, Electromagnetic Recordings/Harvest, 2014).

The Gallery of Horrors

Along with reverence for other peoples' work, a certain amount of irreverence for our own can be a helpful tonic to our creative health and vigor. Here is one humorous songwriter life list that I maintain, to help me stay loose and playful as a songwriter, and especially in co-writing.

Supposedly, late in his career, the composer Leonard Bernstein became creatively paralyzed. Every time he sat down at the piano to compose, he felt the stultifying pressure of knowing that whatever he came up with needed to be "worthy of Leonard Bernstein." This cautionary tale reflects the following profound insight: *Taking ourselves too damn seriously* can definitely get us stuck. One remedy I've developed for my version of the Bernstein Syndrome is a "little list I've got": my *Gallery of Horrors*. Whenever I come up with a real howler—a spectacularly terrible line—instead of throwing it away and trying to forget I ever wrote it, I add it to this list.

I think of this list as primarily a tool for co-writing. (I suppose you could add to your Gallery of Horrors from your own solo work, but it's not nearly as fun—it's a bit like trying to tickle yourself.) In a co-writing session, when you realize you've generated a true clunker, you get to make a joke of it and ceremoniously add it to your Gallery. You thus demonstrate your spontaneity and willingness to edit, your ability to laugh at yourself and leave your ego at the door. You also make it more likely that you and your co-writers will find your way to the occasional magic that waits behind the door of the silly.

I remember the day my Gallery of Horrors became one of my official lists. I was in a three-way co-writing session down in Nashville, writing with Jon Weisberger, a good friend and frequent co-writer of mine; and Jim VanCleve, a great bluegrass fiddler, songwriter, and producer (playing at the time with the band Mountain Heart), with whom I'd never written before.

Jon is a walking encyclopedia of bluegrass music, with an unerring sense for what works in the idiom and what breaks the conventions. Yet he's also sort of a "Northern boy" like me—with a background in journalism and creative writing—thus a safe person for me to take chances with. I can throw any silly line at him, knowing he'll laugh, and that it won't make it into the song if it stinks, but I won't lose cred in his eyes. (Jimmy, on the other hand, I was not so sure about!)

We'd backed ourselves into a corner. We'd started with a musical idea, a harmonically edgy waltz. We wrote music for a verse, then the chorus, and then, inspired by the musical ideas, a third part, likely destined to be a bridge. Now we had three musical sections we really liked, in part because they were so contrastive in feel and mood. Which now meant that no concept or lyric idea we came up seemed to work for *all* those sections!

Finally, after struggling to find a lyric that fit, I heard myself volunteering this sparkling gem:

I was a dolphin, riding the waves
In a sea the color of love

Even as I spoke the line I knew I'd reached a watershed in my career: a truly, spectacularly bad line! We looked around the table silently for a few seconds, then exploded in laughter. I flipped to a back page of my journal and, then and there, inscribed the line proudly and prominently at the top of a new page. And thus was my official "Gallery of Horrors" born.

As it happens, we never did get a lyric we liked for that song. It *did* become a co-written instrumental, which Jim VanCleve recorded as "Grey Afternoon" (on his solo release *No Apologies*, Rural Rhythm Records, 2006).

Recently, Jon told me with some satisfaction that he'd just added a line to his own Gallery of Horrors. "And it's an honest line," he said. "It truly came out of a co-writing session as a serious line for consideration." This is an essential rule of the game for your Gallery of Horrors. It's cheating to just deliberately make up silly or stupid lines for their own sake in order to fill up your Gallery. To make it into your Gallery, each earwax-flavored Every Flavor Bean (apologies to Dumbledore!) must be bagged "in the wild." That is: at the moment you think of—and speak—the line, you must for at least one fleeting moment briefly entertain the notion it might work in the song. (And you never know: you might turn out to be right!) Only after disbelieving groans from your co-writer, or after your own good taste kicks in, do you get to proudly add your new trophy to your Gallery.

Turning Life Lists Back into Songs

Life lists are tools that help you work on expanding and refining your craft. Like prompts (or in some cases, counter-prompts), they can be used for new creative self-challenges: to steal fire from a favorite song, or to write a song that avoids certain go-to habits you have caught yourself depending on too much. But on occasion, as with a song seed collage, you can also turn an entire life list into a single song.

For example, at the end of my days, on my deathbed, I intend to put all my Gallery of Horror lines into one final song to be entitled, "The Worst Song I Ever Wrote (After Which I Died)." I won't try this any sooner; the song might be enough to finally make me kick the bucket. Just think—each of us can write a song like this, and it will take us our whole life to do it!

On a more serious—maybe somber—note, I like to think that, after I'm gone, my Seeds Central will be published as a single tome: my *Posthumous Compendium of Seeds Never Turned into Songs*. As I use up seeds by writing songs from them, they are pulled out of this book. But at any point—if it turns out to be my day to kick the bucket, leaving undone whatever's still on my Bucket List—whatever is left over in Seeds Central will get turned into this book, to inspire fellow songwriters or at least elicit guffaws of derision (my Gallery of Horrors will be in there, after all). I hope you don't find this thought ghoulish: personally, I find it strangely comforting.

FINAL THOUGHTS: YOUR FUTURE BIOGRAPHERS

Beethoven's notebooks are priceless. Every sketch of a banal melody that he eventually worked into masterpieces such as the *Eroica* symphony provides precious data for musicians and scholars in subsequent centuries, to learn not only about his work and process, but about the nature of creativity in general. To manage your own creative workflow most effectively, you need the humility to know you are not Beethoven, Woody Guthrie, Hank Williams, or Bob Dylan—yet! Still, you want to respect your work and its potential enough, and be curious enough about the magical work of songwriting itself, to retain your own materials as if—someday—someone else might be interested. I call this "being kind to Your Future Biographers." It's a strange, yet ultimately liberating attitude, humble yet presumptuous—celebrating imperfection, courting perfection, and honoring the Muse, all the while loving every step of your songwriter's journey.

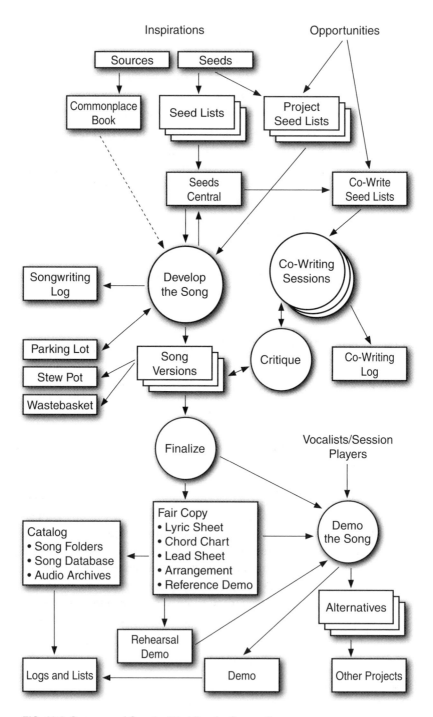

FIG. 10.2. Summary of Creative Workflow for Songwriting

GLOSSARY

The following glossary provides short definitions of terms used in the book. Some are familiar terms, such as "inspiration" or "opportunity," used in fairly specific ways relevant to the book's context and scope—creative workflow management in songwriting. For example, while all sorts of artistic forms might involve creative workflow, here we presume a songwriting context, and generally will not indicate that explicitly in the terms used.

A few terms are carried over from my earlier book, *Songwriting Strategies: A 360° Approach* (indicated with [*SWS*]). And a few terms, such as "Stewpot" and "morsel," intended to be humorous, metaphorical, and/or fanciful, are indicated with [fanciful]. While these terms may seem whimsical, the practices they name are serious in intent. I encourage you to choose and personalize your own terms for these and other work products and activities, as you continue to refine your own creative workflow and songwriter's practice.

activity. Work done directly with creative material drawn from or transformed into work products as part of writing songs, as well as supporting tasks such as sorting and organizing, inventorying, maintaining logs of work done, etc.

annotations. Various ways of marking creative material (lyrics, chord or melody, etc.) with indications for alternatives, evaluations, or process reflections. These can be useful for continuity across writing sessions (solo or co-write), and across versions.

appointments. [fanciful] Used metaphorically in this context for appointments you make with *yourself* (as opposed to driven by a specific business opportunity) to work regularly— at scheduled times, and for scheduled durations—with various resources of your creative workflow. Appointments facilitate use of primarily inspiration-driven resources (such as Seeds Central), in a more task-driven way, and thus form key components of your overall songwriter's practice.

For example: in an Appointment with Inspiration (AWI), you work with a seed drawn from a particular song seed list—especially Seeds Central. For an Appointment with Greatness, you might schedule time to work creatively with a song from your Songs I Wish I'd Written list.

commonplace book. [fanciful] Complementary to a seeds list, a container for *source* material.

creative material. Material in any *facet*—rhythmic, lyrical, melodic, harmonic, or combinations thereof—generated or compiled with the intent of incorporating it in a song, as well as supporting materials created or used in the process of creating the song.

creative workflow. Workflow of creative materials used in activities, and yielding work products, involved with songwriting. *Creative* workflow is distinct from workflow involving, for example, business tasks. Also, creative *workflow* can be distinguished from creative *activity* (e.g., private musical experience, or interactions in co-writing and collaboration) that does not involve creating or transforming work products.

draft. A relatively complete material for a song in at least one facet. For example, a draft of just lyrics for a song would generally have material for multiple sections.

facet. [*SWS*] One of the core elements of creative material involved in songwriting: rhythmic, lyrical, melodic, or harmonic material.

fair copy. A song version intended to be a definitive reference source for the song, created as part of final revisions for the song.

inspiration. Seed or source material, captured in some form, with the intent of using it as a starting point for developing a song.

journal end pages. A formatting strategy for catching seeds in the context of other songwriting work, by documenting them outside specific session pages in *end pages* of the journal. End pages can be filled with seed material working back to front.

morsel. A fragment of creative material pulled out of a song during drafting or revision that is deemed worth keeping on hand, with respect to a possible different usage for the material. Morsels should go in your *Stewpot* specifically if you believe they could be of creative use in *another* song (generally, not one written yet). As they are pulled out of a song in development, they will generally have context that needs to be stripped away to use them elsewhere.

opportunity. A possibility for *placement* of a song. Responding to an opportunity might involve searching your catalog for an existing song or writing a new song responsive to the requirements and constraints (timeframe, etc.) of the opportunity.

Parking Lot. [fanciful] A container for creative material for the current song, that needs to be dealt with in a non-linear manner. As part of finishing a session or revision, and definitely as part of finalizing the song, the parking lot should be "cleaned out"—diverting material, if not back into the song ultimately, then to the *Stewpot* or the *wastebasket*.

placement. Getting a song published, recorded, performed, or incorporated into some other project context (e.g., placement in a film or television synchronization usage).

project-specific seed list. A seed list tied to a specific task or project—as opposed to general seed lists such as Seeds Central. Coordinating access to a project-specific seed list is a touch-point between creative workflow and task or project management.

revision. A draft representing a distinct, consecutive iteration of the song. A revision might add, change, or delete material from an earlier revision. Deleted material might be temporarily in the Parking Lot, but then would typically get resolved at the end of the writing session, or when the revision is settled. Deleted material deemed of possible value for another song context can be removed (as a *morsel*) to the *Stewpot*. Otherwise, deleted material, in effect, is relegated to the *wastebasket*; however, it might still be accessible (if indirectly) in a preserved earlier version.

scan-and-match. An activity where a resource such as a *song seed list* (or other interim work product such as a worksheet) is scanned—moved through consecutively—until an item judged responsive to a specific creative situation is found. Scan-and-match can be used in solo or co-writing, and often involves testing a pre-collected group of resources for a good match with a specific song situation, for example: looking through a list of titles in response to an instrumental track, or looking for a chord progression providing sufficient contrast for a bridge section of a song. Unlike seed sweeps, scan-and-match can usually halt as soon as a qualifying seed or other resource is found.

seed sweep. [fanciful] The activity of working entirely through a given seed list to cull a list of multiple seeds matching some criterion.

sketch. A first step in developing song material, usually (though not always) in response to a seed or source as a starting point, involving material in one or more facets. Sketches may include only a fragment of the eventual form of the song, and may include multiple iterations.

song journal. A consecutive and chronological journal (usually physical or hard copy) for working on songs in a series of sessions.

song seed notebook. A container that facilitates catching seeds in an immediate fashion in the midst of everyday (non-songwriting) activity. The notebook might contain seeds as well as other material, and you might have several concurrent notebooks for seed catching in different contexts.

song seed. [SWS] A single, fragmentary creative material identified as a potential starting point for a song.

songwriter life list. [fanciful] A list you accumulate over time, consisting of fragments of your own or other peoples' material linked thematically in some way. Like a seed or source list, but generally added to in a purposeful way, sometimes as a result of processing seed lists. Also, worked with in a different way than seed lists: either as guides and challenges for working on craft, or for special creative projects.

song/co-writing log. A work product for capturing reflec-tions and process history about particular songs and co-writes.

songwriting practice. Managing your overall work as a songwriter, including creative workflow as well as management of business aspects of the profession.

source. [complementary term to *seed*] Material not created by the songwriter, used as input to the songwriting process. When source material is incorporated directly into the song, it is generally essential to track and acknowledge provenance of the source. It may also be necessary to clear license for usage, from a legal or contractual standpoint.

Stewpot. [fanciful] A container for fragments of creative material (*morsels*) pulled out of a draft or version of a song. Frag-ments go in the Stewpot if you believe they could be of crea-tive use in *other* songs. Since they are pulled out of a song in development, they will have context that needs to be stripped away to use them elsewhere.

stub. A placeholder indicating primarily the presence or inten-ded location of a given section in the song section, before material for that section has been sketched or drafted. The stub might include a brief *annotation* about the desired content for the missing section.

supporting materials. Materials created in support of the song-writing process, not likely to be incorporated directly into the song. (While sometimes called *pre-writing* materials, such material may be generated at any point in the process, including later in revision.)

wastebasket. [fanciful] A "virtual" container for material not saved as part of creative workflow. In many circumstances, you need not actively *delete* material to relegate it to the wastebasket. It is moved there by virtue of being deleted from a later revision, and not otherwise saved (e.g., in the *Stewpot*). It may still remain accessible in a prior version.

work product. Any physical or digital "container" for creative material.

workflow management. Established regular practices involving songwriting activities and work products, that make the songwriting process as a whole more effective.

ABOUT THE AUTHOR

Photo by Louise Bichan

Mark Simos, associate professor of songwriting at Berklee College of Music in Boston, is an acclaimed songwriter and composer who combines a deep grounding in varied traditional styles with continuing willingness to explore, innovate, and stretch musical boundaries. More than 150 of Mark's songs and instrumentals have been recorded by prominent roots, Americana, and bluegrass artists, including Laurie Lewis and Tom Rozum, Alison Krauss and Union Station, Ricky Skaggs, the Del McCoury Band, and the Infamous Stringdusters, among many others. He has collaborated with a diverse range of artists and writers, from singer-songwriter Catie Curtis to Australian rock icon Jimmy Barnes on his *Rage and Ruin* album.

As a teacher at Berklee since 2006, Mark has created innovative curriculum for songwriting, focusing on creative process, guitar techniques for songwriters, co-writing and collaboration, and protocols for listener-centered peer critique. He documented key elements of his holistic approach in *Songwriting Strategies: A 360° Approach* (Berklee Press, 2014), now used as a text in college songwriting courses in the U.S. and internationally. He also contributed the chapter "The Performing Songwriter's Dilemma: Principles and Practices" in the *Singer-Songwriter Handbook* (ed. Justin Williams and Katherine Williams, Bloomsbury Publishing, 2017). As lead faculty facilitator for Berklee's Songs for Social Change initiative, he is committed to inspiring and empowering songwriters to lend their artistic voices to those issues and causes they believe in most deeply.

Mark is also a respected fiddler, accompanist, and "tunesmith"— a composer of new dance tunes in traditional forms—in varied Celtic and American roots musical idioms. His songs and "traditional tunes from imaginary countries" bring a contemporary sensibility to timeless forms, with a distinctive signature of surprising turns of melody and harmony, and intricately crafted lyrics.

Mark has performed in concerts and festivals, led workshops, and served on staff at music programs and camps in the U.S., Europe, and Australia. In addition to an acclaimed solo song-cycle album, *Crazy Faith*, Mark has released four albums of original and traditional fiddle music, and has been featured on numerous recordings as a guitar accompanist for renowned traditional players, including Brian Conway, Fintan Vallely, and April Verch, among others. At Berklee, Mark founded the Appalachian Old-Time Ensemble, and has mentored many talented musicians in the American Roots Music Program in the tunesmith's art.

INDEX

A Modern Method for Guitar – Volume 1
by William Leavitt
Now this renowned method is available with online video access to fourteen hours of instruction from Larry Baione, chair of Berklee's guitar department!
00137387 Book/Online Video $24.99

The Contemporary Singer – 2nd Edition
by Anne Peckham
Topics covered include getting started, posture, belting and diction, maintaining vocal health, microphone technique, and much more.
50449595 Book/Online Audio...................$24.99

Berklee Jazz Standards for Solo Piano
by Robert Christopherson, Hey Rim Jeon, Ross Ramsay, Tim Ray
Twelve arrangements for solo jazz piano of standard jazz tunes. These arrangements are fun to play and musically suitable for performance.
00160482 Book/Online Audio...................$19.99

Berklee Jazz Drums
by Casey Scheuerell
Learn to develop your own sound, perform a wide variety of essential jazz time feels, and improvise dynamic fills and solos, taught in the tradition of Alan Dawson and other Berklee luminaries of drum education.
50449612 Book/Online Audio...................$19.99

Understanding Audio – 2nd Edition
by Dan Thompson
Explore the fundamentals of audio and acoustics that impact every stage of the music recording process.
00148197 Book $24.99

Music Composition for Film and Television
by Lalo Schifrin
Lalo Schifrin shares his insights into the intimate relationship between music and drama.
50449604 Book $34.99

Arranging for Strings
by Mimi Rabson
This book presents time-tested technique and contemporary developments in writing and arranging for strings. You'll learn strategies for authentic writing in many different styles and find ideas to take you personal sound forward. Discover voicings that work best for each project and explore the intricacies of bowing. Hear articulation approaches from pads to chopping in the online audio examples.
00190207 Book/Online Audio.......................$19.99

Music Law in the Digital Age – 2nd Edition
by Allen Bargfrede
This cutting-edge, plain-language guide shows you how copyright law drives the contemporary music industry.
00148196 Book............................$19.99

The Berklee Book of Jazz Harmony
by Joe Mulholland & Tom Hojnacki
This text provides a strong foundation in harmonic principles, supporting further study in jazz composition, arranging, and improvisation.
00113755 Book/Online Audio...................$27.50

Berklee Contemporary Music Notation
by Jonathan Feist
This reference presents a comprehensive look at contemporary music notation. You will learn the meaning and stylistic practice for many types of notation that are currently in common use.
00202547 Book............................$16.99

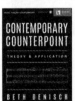

Contemporary Counterpoint: Theory & Application
by Beth Denisch
Use counterpoint to make your music more engaging and creative. You will learn "tricks of the trade" from the masters and apply these skills to contemporary styles.
00147050 Book/Audio Online...................$19.99

Songwriting Strategies
A 360-Degree Approach
by Mark Simos
Write songs starting from any direction: melody, lyric, harmony, rhythm, or idea. This book will help you expand your range and flexibility as a songwriter.
50449621 Book............................$22.99